**M.M. Publications Ltd.,**
P.B. No. 226, Kottayam, Pin - 686 001.
Kerala, India.  Tel : 0481 - 2563721 - 22-23
Fax: ++91- 481 - 2564393
E mail: subscription@mmp.in
childrensdivision@mmp.in

**NEW DELHI:** Malayala Manorama Co. Ltd.,
Andhra Vanitha Mandali Building, 2, Azad Bhavan
Road, Indraprastha Estate,  New Delhi - 110002.
Phone: 011- 23379718,  23379719,  23379720
**MUMBAI:** Malayala Manorama,
A-404 Marathon Innova, A Wing 4th Floor,
Off. Ganpat Rao Kadam Marg, Opp. Peninsula
Corporate Park, Lower Parel (West),
Mumbai- 400 013. Tel: 022 - 24911693 /
24900523 / 24901331 / 24912381
**KOLKATA:** Malayala Manorama,
14 Parasar Road, Near Lake Market,
Kolkata - 700 029.  Tel: 033 - 24198233, 24198048
Fax : 033 - 24198048
**PATNA:** Malayala Manorama,
608, Jagat Trade Centre, Frazar Road,
Patna-800 001.          Tel: 0612 - 2233809
**JAIPUR:** Malayala Manorama,
C/o Royal business Centre, Usha Plaza Building,
Near Jaipur Tower, M.I. Road, Jaipur - 302 001.
Tel: 0141 - 2368360,      Mob: 94616 28972
**HYDERABAD:** Malayala Manorama,
C/o Dr. B.C. Mathur 8-2-629/1/B, Road No.12,
Banjara Hills, Hyderabad - 500 034.
Tel: 040 - 23314168,   23324692
Fax: 040 - 23322970
**BANGALORE:** Malayala Manorama,
No. 132, Kantha Court, 3rd Floor, Lal Baugh Road,
Bangalore - 560 027.     Tel: 22247735 / 36
**CHENNAI:** Malayala Manorama,
2nd Floor, # 748, Anna Salai, Chennai-600 002.
Tel: 28542607 (Circulation-Direct), 28542601
to 06 (Board Line) Fax: ++ 91- 044 - 28542611
18004252607 (Toll free)
**COIMBATORE:** Malayala Manorama,
101, Sunshine Buildings, 1056, Avinashi Road,
Opp. Nilgiri Super Market, Coimbatore - 641 018.
Tel: 2241911 / 2245470          Fax: 2245367
**LUCKNOW:** Malayala Manorama, B-1657,
Indira Nagar, Lucknow-226 016. Tel: 0522-2341576
**CHANDIGARH:** Malayala Manorama,
H No. 1824, Top Floor, Sector 22-B,
Chandigarh -160 022.
Tel: 0172 - 2724699          Mob: 09417310727
**BHOPAL:** Malayala Manorama, Plot No.161,
Gopal Bhawan, Zone 1, M.P. Nagar, Bhopal.
Tel. 0755 - 2557937
**THIRUVANANTHAPURAM:**
Malayala Manorama, P.B. No. 160,
Thampanoor East, Thiruvananthapuram- 695 001.
Tel: 2328198          Fax: ++ 91 - 471 - 2327886
**COCHIN:** P.B. No. 5008, Malayala Manorama
Bldgs, Panampilly Nagar, Cochin - 682 036, Kerala.
Tel: 0484- 2316285   Fax:++91- 484 - 2315745

MANORAMA
# TELL ME WHY

● April 2012 ● Volume : 6 ● No : 7

## States of India

When a united, independent India was born, it was not without pains. Before the British left, our great country was divided into a large number of provinces, many of them under the rule of local princes. The Himalayan task of joining all the diverse regions of India to form a strong united nation fell upon Sardar Vallabhai Patel, who was known as the 'iron man of India'. He was assisted by V.P. Menon, secretary of the Ministry of States. Theirs was indeed a task ridden with challenges, because different provincial kingdoms reacted differently to the appeal. Though Cochin joined the union easily, in Hyderabad, the Indian Army had to tackle the Nizam's army before receiving a 'yes'.

Later, the nation was divided into a number of states based on their languages. Through all these birth pangs, a great nation was being born, ready to make its presence felt in the modern world and create history. This issue of Tell Me Why tells about our states.

The sketches of places given in this issue are not drawn to scale, and not maps drawn according to cartographic norms. The boundaries are not to scale, and may not be accurate.

FROM THE HOUSE OF MAGIC POT, MANORAMA YEAR BOOK, VANITHA, THE WEEK AND THE MALAYALA MANORAMA DAILY

For subscription enquiries: Please call our toll-free number - **1800 4255 002** (between 9 to 5 on working days)
To subscribe to Tell Me Why online, logon to **www.manoramaonline.com/subscribe**

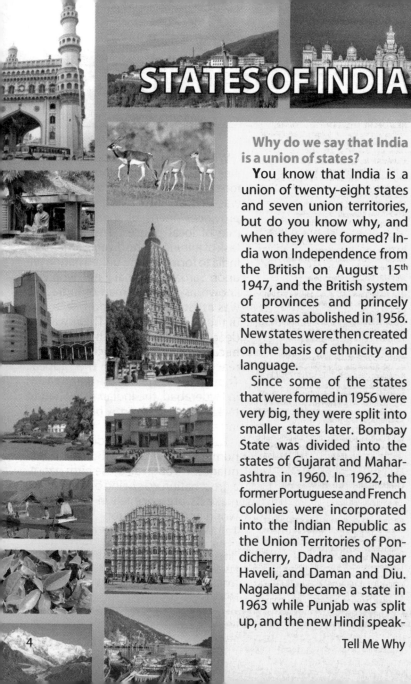

# STATES OF INDIA

**Why do we say that India is a union of states?**

You know that India is a union of twenty-eight states and seven union territories, but do you know why, and when they were formed? India won Independence from the British on August 15th 1947, and the British system of provinces and princely states was abolished in 1956. New states were then created on the basis of ethnicity and language.

Since some of the states that were formed in 1956 were very big, they were split into smaller states later. Bombay State was divided into the states of Gujarat and Maharashtra in 1960. In 1962, the former Portuguese and French colonies were incorporated into the Indian Republic as the Union Territories of Pondicherry, Dadra and Nagar Haveli, and Daman and Diu. Nagaland became a state in 1963 while Punjab was split up, and the new Hindi speak-

ing state of Haryana was formed in 1966.

The year 1971 saw Himachal Pradesh become a state, while Manipur, Meghalaya, and Tripura became states the next year. The Kingdom of Sikkim joined the India Union in 1975, while Arunachal Pradesh and Mizoram became states in 1987, followed by Goa.

The year 2000 saw the creation of three new states – Chattisgarh, Uttaranchal, and Jharkhand.

Oh, you are from United States of America? I am from United States of India!

States of India

# Andhra Pradesh

Capital : **Hyderabad**
Districts : **23**
Principal Languages : **Telugu and Urdu**
State Bird : **Indian Roller**
State Animal : **Blackbuck**
State Flower : **Water Lily**

**Why is the history of Andhra Pradesh fascinating?**

Over the centuries, Andhra Pradesh has been ruled by several great dynasties, including the Satavahanas, Sakas, Ikshvakus, Eastern Chalukyas and the Kakatiyas. After the end of the Kakatiya dynasty, a few local kingdoms rose to power in different parts of the kingdom. Among these, the Vijaynagar kingdom was the most powerful one. In the 16th century, the state saw the emergence of the Qutb Shahi dynasty which was defeated by the Mughals. In 1707, Hyderabad came under the rule of the Nizams.

After independence, Andhra Pradesh became the first state to be formed on the basis of language. The Telugu speaking people were given twenty-one districts, out of which nine were in the Nizam's dominions, and the rest in the Madras Presidency. However following

*Lepakshi Nandi -A Huge Statue in Andhra Pradesh*

Tell Me Why

*Visakhapatnam - Seaport*

## Why is the geography of Andhra Pradesh important?

Andhra Pradesh is located in South India, bounded by Tamil Nadu in the south, Maharashtra in the north and northwest, Madhya Pradesh and Orissa in the northeast, Karnataka in the west, and by the Bay of Bengal in the east. It is situated on the Deccan plateau, and is one of the oldest geological formations of the country. The Godavari and Krishna rivers cut through the state, forming large deltas before joining the Bay of Bengal.

The state can be divided into three important regions based on its geography - the coastal region, the interior region, known as Rayalseema, and the Telengana region, and nine adjoining districts. Andhra Pradesh has a wide variety of wildlife and has natural beauty. The state is home to India's largest tiger reserve, in the Nallamala forest.

an agitation in 1953, eleven districts of the Madras state were taken to form a new Andhra state with Kurnool as its capital. Nine districts under the Nizam were later added to form the enlarged state of Andhra Pradesh in 1956.

States of India

*Charminar*

He's a Hitech man working in HITECH city!

**Why is Kuchipudi considered Andhra Pradesh's gift to the world?**

Kuchipudi is a classical dance form from Andhra Pradesh. It is known for its graceful movements, strong narrative, and dramatic character. The credit for the existing dance form of Kuchipudi goes to Siddhendra Yogi. The style is a blend of folk and classical dance.

Kuchipudi dance drama has a perfect blend of rhythm, mime, and pure dance. This art form has some very complicated items of original footwork such as tracing out an outline of a lion or an elephant with the feet on the floor, or dancing with the feet on the edges of a circular brass tray, or with a water pot,

delicately and precariously balanced on the head.

Kuchipudi flourished as a dramatic form of dance for

*Kuchipudi*

8

*HITEC City*

acres of land in the suburbs of Hyderabad. This technology township has made Hyderabad and Andhra Pradesh one of the most important centres for the information technology industry in the world.

hundreds of years. It was held in high esteem by the rulers of the Deccan, and is today considered to be Andhra Pradesh's gift to the world of arts.

Dhamak Dhumak Dhom...

Wow! This Guinness book is dedicated to Andhra Pradesh!

LIBRARY

**Why is Andhra Pradesh called the state of Guinness records?**

Andhra Pradesh has won Guinness records in many fields. It has India's largest and Asia's second largest road cum railway bridge at Rajahmundry, and the state owned Road Transport Corporation is the largest bus operator in the world. In cinema, it holds the record for the largest film production facility in the world, while Dr. Brahmanandam holds the record for acting in the most number of Telugu films in the role of a comedian. D. Ramanaidu is listed as the most prolific producer, while 2800 kuchipudi dancers performed kuchipudi to create another Guinness record. Recently, a huge 5,570-kg 'laddu' prepared for the recent Ganesh festival in Andhra Pradesh also entered the Guinness world records!

# Arunachal Pradesh

Capital : **Itanagar**
Districts : **16**
Official Language : **English**
State Bird : **Great Hornbill**
State Animal : **Gayal (Mithun)**
State Flower : **Foxtail Orchid**

**Why is Arunachal Pradesh called the 'land of Himalayan mountains?'**

Arunachal Pradesh means 'land of the dawn-lit mountains,' in Sanskrit. Much of Arunachal Pradesh is covered by the Himalayas. However, parts of Lohit, Changlang and Tirap are covered by the Patkai hills. Kangto, Nyegi Kangsang, the main Gorichen peak, and the Eastern Gorichen peak are some of the highest peaks in this region of the Himalayas.

At the lowest elevations, you will find semi-evergreen forests. Much of the state consists of Eastern Himalayan broadleaf forests. Towards the northern border with China, with increasing elevation, comes a mixture of Eastern and Northeastern Himalayan sub-alpine conifer forests, followed by Eastern Himalayan alpine shrub and meadows. Finally, there is just rock and ice on the highest peaks.

*Arunachal Pradesh-*
*The Landscape*

10

*Itanagar, Capital of Arunachal Pradesh*

*Tawang Monastery in Arunachal Pradesh*

**Why is the history of Arunachal Pradesh said to be full of myths and legends?**

The history of Arunachal Pradesh is rich in myths and legends. The land is mentioned in the literature of Kalika Purana and Mahabharata. This place is the Prabhu Mountains of Puranas. It was here that the sage Parashuram atoned for his sins, and the sage Vyasa meditated. This was the land where King Bhismaka founded his kingdom, and Lord Krishna married his consort Rukmini.

The recorded history of Arunachal Pradesh is available only from the sixteenth century onwards. Its modern history begins with the imposition of the British rule in Assam in 1826. Before 1962, Arunachal was popularly called the North Eastern Frontier Agency and was constitutionally a part of Assam. The Ministry of External Affairs administered it until 1965, and subsequently, the Ministry of Home Affairs, through the Governor of Assam. In 1972, it was constituted as a Union Territory, and renamed Arunachal Pradesh. On 20th February in 1987, it became the 24th state of the Indian Union.

Sage Vyasa meditated here.

## Why is the culture of Arunachal Pradesh unique?

**A**runachal Pradesh has a great cultural background, and its people celebrate numerous festivals round the year, together with their own set of rituals, music and dance. The state has 20 major tribes, and numerous sub-tribes living in the villages across the state. Different tribal groups have their own set of beliefs and notions about their religion. The people of Arunachal Pradesh form three cultural groups, and each group practices its own religion. The people of the first group are usually Buddhists, while people of the second group practice Donyi Poloism or worship of the Sun and Moon Gods. Christianity and Hinduism. The third group practices Christianity and Hinduism.

The people of Arunachal make beautiful masks, and periodically stage pantomimes and masked dances. They specialize in carving semi-religious motifs on wood, and make exquisite carpets, painted wooden vessels, and silver articles. They are expert workers in cane and bamboo, and weave articles that they commonly use in their daily lives like shawls, jackets, shoulder bags, and coats. Specific tribes have crafts exclusive to their area of expertise.

*A Statue of Buddha in Tawang, Arunachal Pradesh*

# Assam

Capital : **Dispur**
Districts : **27**
Principal Languages : **Assamese, Bodo, Kari**
State Bird : **White-winged Wood Duck**
State Animal : **One-horned Rhino**
State Flower : **Foxtail Orchid**

## How is Assam divided geographically?

**A**ssam is located at the gateway of Northeast India. It is surrounded by states like Arunachal Pradesh in the North, Nagaland in the east, Mizoram and Tripura in the south, and West Bengal in the west. Assam can be broadly divided into three distinct physical units, the Brahmaputra Valley in the north, the Barak Valley in the narrow protruding south, and the state's hilly region separating the two valleys. Assam has stunning scenic grandeur, with dense tracts of tropical for-

*River Brahmaputra*

ests, interspersed with emerald patchwork quilts of paddy, and lush tea gardens enriched by the flow of the Brahmaputra River. The alluvial plains of the Assam valley enjoy an abundance of natural riches. The state is the largest producer of timber and tea in the country, and it has the oldest oil refinery in India. Did you know that Assam is the only region in the world that has its own variety of tea, called Camellia Assamica?

I like this rich and strong Assam tea, imported from USA!

**CURIOUS FACT**

**Assam Tea**

**Assam** has a tea named after it- the Camellia Assamica. This tea is known for a full-bodied flavour and strong bright colour. The tea leaves originate from bushes in the Assam Valley in India, where the Brahmaputra river flows. The river has deposited a rich loam over the valley, and the area experiences both hot monsoon seasons and cool, dry winters, which are ideal conditions for the Assam tea bush. Assam tea is very popular as a 'breakfast tea'.

## When was Assam formed?

**T**he ancient land of Assam was known as 'Kamarupa' or 'Pragjyotish' in the epics. The early history of Assam is believed to be of the Varman dynasty. The reign of this dynasty extended from 400 AD to the 13th century. By the 15th century, the kingdoms of Ahom and Koch were established. In the later part of the 18th century, the Ahom Kingdom was weakened due to internal strife. The Burmese seized power, which prompted the British to intervene. The British subdued the Burmese, and set out to organize the administration, as well as to improve transport and communication.

After Indian Independence, Assam witnessed several separations of territories. Arunachal Pradesh, Nagaland, Meghalaya, and Mizoram were all carved out of Assam, and became separate states over the years.

*Bihu Dance*

## Why is Assam said to be rich in culture?

Assam is the meeting ground of different cultures. The state has a large number of tribes, each unique in its tradition, culture, dress, and exotic way of life. From time immemorial, the people of Assam have traditionally been craftsmen. Artists, sculptors, masons, weavers, spinners, potters, goldsmiths, and workers of ivory, wood, bamboo, cane and hide have flourished in Assam from ancient times. Weaving is a traditional craft that every Assamese woman takes pride in. The Assamese women produce silk, and cotton cloth of exquisite designs in their looms. Assam is renowned for its exquisite silks including the world famous Muga silk.

To sum up, Assamese culture is a rich blend of ethnic practices and ancient beliefs.

I have no more teeth to give you for your ornaments!

# Bihar

Capital : **Patna**
Districts : **37**
Principal Languages : **Hindi, Urdu**
State Bird : **Indian Roller**
State Animal : **Gaur**
State Flower : **White Orchid-tree**

*Mahabodhi Temple*

## Why do we say that Bihar has a magnificent history?

Bihar has seen the birth of ancient civilizations and modern Indian history. Hindu, Buddhist, Jain, Muslim and Sikh shrines abound in this ancient land, where India's first major empire rose and fell. Bihar is the land of not only great religious preachers, but also of mighty emperors and valiant warriors. Ancient Bihar was known as Magadha, and was the centre of power, learning, and culture in India for 1000 years. India's first empire, the Mauryan Empire, as well as one of the world's great religions, Buddhism, arose in what is now Bihar. One of the first known republics in the world, Licchavi existed in the region. The classical Gupta dynasty of Bihar was known to have been a period of great culture and learning, and is, in fact, called the Golden Age of India.

During the medieval period, except for the brief period of Sher Shah's reign, the province of Bihar never enjoyed the status of an independent state.

Tell Me Why

16

### How can we describe the geography of Bihar?

**B**ihar is located in the eastern part of the country. It lies midway between West Bengal in the east, and Uttar Pradesh in the west. It is bounded by Nepal in the north, and by Jharkhand in the south. The Bihar plain is divided into two unequal halves by the river Ganga, which flows through the middle, from West to East.

Bihar is mainly a vast stretch of very fertile flat land. It can be grouped into three regions. They are the northern mountainous region, the Indo-Gangetic Plain and the Southern Plain. Many rivers like the Ganga, Kosi, Kamla, Burhi Gandak, Saryu and others flow through the state. The Bapabar Hills, Mandargiri Hills are some of the mountains in the state.

*Patna,*
*Capital of Bihar*

In 1652, the British started business from Patna, and soon they took over Bihar. The British ruled Bihar from 1765 to 1947.

When India became independent, Bihar became a state under the Union of India. In 2000, the state of Jharkhand was carved out of Bihar.

*Ruins of the Ancient City of Vaishali*

**Why are festivals in Bihar a reflection of the culture and traditions of the people?**

Bihar is steeped in history, and has a rich tradition of festivals. The most famous festival is Chhatth Puja, which is celebrated twice a year. Sama-Chakeva is another festival celebrated in Bihar, especially in Mithila. Navarathri is a ten day festival where the people of Bihar worship Goddess Durga for nine days. On the tenth day, the idol of the goddess is taken to the river and cast into it. Maker Sankranti marks the end of winter, and the beginning of the summer season. Mahavir Jayanti, which is celebrated with great pomp, and Deo Diwali which marks the final liberation of Lord Mahavira, are important Jain festivals in Bihar. Ramnavami, Nagpanchami, Bihula are some of the other festivals celebrated in Bihar.

### Mahatma Gandhi Setu

The **Mahatma Gandhi Setu** (bridge) over the river Ganga in Patna is India's longest river bridge. The bridge spans over 5.575 km from Hajipur at the north end, to Patna at the south end. Before the bridge was constructed, people who wanted to go to the north of Bihar, had to cross the river using boats or small ships, steamers or take a longer rail route. The bridge was inaugurated in May 1982 by the then Prime Minister, Mrs. Indira Gandhi.

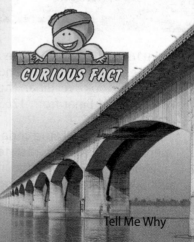

CURIOUS FACT

# Chhattisgarh

Capital : **Raipur**
Districts : **18**
Principal Languages : **Hindi, Chhattisgarhi**
State Bird : **Hill Myna**
State Animal : **Wild Buffalo**

## Why is Chhattisgarh a new state with an ancient history?

In ancient times, Chhattisgarh was called Dakshin Kosala. According to mythology, Ram stayed in Dakshin Kosala during his exile. Later, Chhattisgarh remained part of every empire that ruled the country, right from the days of the great Magadha Empire. The English recognized the mineral wealth of the land, and established a vast network of mines and railway track throughout the area. This marked the beginning of a new phase in the region's history. In recent times, the state of Chhattisgarh has been carved out of Madhya Pradesh to become the 26th state of the Indian Union on November 1st 2000.

*Chitrakot Waterfalls, Chhattisgarh*

*Vivekananda Sarovar*

## Why is Chhattisgarh called a 'land of opportunity'?

Chhattisgarh has been called a land of opportunity because the state has immense mineral and forest resources. Substantial deposits of limestone, iron-ore, copper-ore, rock phosphate, manganese-ore, bauxite, coal, asbestos and mica exist in the newly formed state. While the availability of coal has helped the state to become a major producer of power, an abundance of iron-ore deposits have helped the setting up of a large number of iron and steel industries. Another big source of income for the state is forest revenue, for 12% of India's forests are in Chhattisgarh. Agriculturally, it is a very fertile area. The soil and climate here are suitable for rice, which is grown here in large quantities. Chhattisgarh supplies food grain to almost 600 rice mills. Did you know that Chhattisgarh is the richest state in terms of mineral wealth? Twenty-Eight varieties of major minerals including diamonds, are found here.

## Why do we say that Chhattisgarh has a colourful culture?

Chhattisgarh boasts of a cultural heritage rich with vibrant dances, melodious music, magnificent arts and crafts, and colourful fairs and festivals. The majority of the state's population belong to tribal communities. The tribal people love to adorn themselves with ornaments made from cowries, beads, shells, bones and feathers. Apart from the tribals, many people of Chhattisgarh actually belong to the neighbouring states.

Chhattisgarh is undoubtedly a reservoir of talent. Since ages, dance and performing arts have been practiced here. While Raut Nacha is the folk dance

20

*A Museum in Chhattisgarh*

of cowherds, Panthi 'Karma' and Soowa dance forms are popular all over the state. Music forms an inseparable part of the state's culture. The rich traditional folk songs that are famous include sohar, bihav, and pathoni. The arts and crafts of Chhattisgarh are truly amazing. Wood carvings, bamboo work and furniture, bell metal handicrafts, figures of terracotta, tribal jewelry, paintings, and clay pieces are some of the specialties from the state.

**Chitrakot Falls**
The Chitrakot Falls is a waterfall located in the Bastar district of Chhattisgarh on the Indravati River. It is about 29 metres high. The breadth varies, as the water level in the river goes down during summer. Most of the area that surround the falls is forest.

*Purkhauti Muktangan - A Museum in Chhattisgarh*

Wow, what a colourful butterfly!

# Goa

Capital : **Panaji**
Districts : **2**
Principal Languages : **Konkani and Marathi**
State Bird : **Black-crested Bulbul**
State Animal : **Indian Bison**

## Why is the history of Goa so special?

The history of Goa goes back to the 3rd century BC. It was the part of Mauryan Empire. Goa has an endless list of rulers who have ruled this state through the ages. The 14th century saw Goa gradually becoming a trading centre with mostly horses being traded with the Middle East. It was at this time that powerful

*Panaji Circle, Goa*

empires took Goa under their rule. However, things started to change in 1510 AD, when the Portuguese arrived in Goa. Owing to its natural harbours, coupled with wide rivers, Goa served as a perfect base for the Portuguese to take control of the spice trade from Middle East. Dur-

*Dona Paula Beach, Goa*

Tell Me Why

ing the time of the spice trade, Goa reached its golden Age, and Old goa became the biggest city in East. Though India earned her independence from British rule in the year 1947, Goa had remained a Portuguese colony. In the year 1961, the former Prime Minister, Jawaharlal Nehru, sent armed forces to Goa. The Indian army took over Goa in just two days. Goa became one of the Union Territories of India, along with Daman and Diu. In 1987, Goa became a separate state, while Daman and Diu were made a separate Union Territory.

## Why is tourism important to Goa?

**T**ourism caught the imagination of the people in the world in the 1980's and Goa, with its natural beauty, coupled with its charming Portuguese influence and culture, became a favorite destination for hordes of tourists from all over the world. Today, Goa is one of the most important tourism destinations in India. The sun kissed beaches, the beautifully adorned churches, the historic forts and unique culture, as well as the unending carnivals and parties all make Goa irresistible, both to the Indian and well as the international tourist.

The pleasant weather of the state throughout the year is one of the major contributors that promote tourism in Goa.

*Goa Coastline*

*A Goan Portuguese Villa*

## How can we describe Goa's geography?

Goa is located on the western coast of India, in the Konkan coastal belt. The state is separated from Maharashtra by the Terekhol River in the north, Karnataka in the south, the Western Ghats in the east, and the Arabian Sea in the West. Goa as a region can be divided into four divisions. They are the Eastern Hill region comprising areas in the Western Ghats, the Central Valley Lands, the Flood Plains comprising the coastal plains and rolling uplands, and the Coastal Plains.

The Sahyadri Ranges are spread over an area of about 600 sq km., with an average elevation of 800 metres. The Central region of Goa has plateaus ranging between altitudes of 30 m to 100 m. The rivers of Mandovi and Zuari drain the major portions of the plains. Goa's coastline is a scenic combination of bays and headlands broken by large estuaries of the Mandovi and Zuari Rivers, coupled with minor streams.

### Mormugao

The city of Mormugao in Goa state is situated on the west coast of India. Mormugao Harbour is very picturesque, and is one of the region's most impressive natural ports. The Port of Mormugao was an important trading centre for the British. It was also the capital of the Portuguese Empire in India.

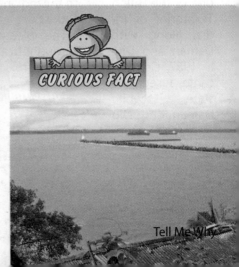

CURIOUS FACT

Tell Me Why

# Gujarat

Capital : **Gandhinagar**
Districts : **26**
Principal Language : **Gujarati**
State Bird : **Greater Flamingo**
State Animal : **Asiatic Lion**
State Flower : **Marigold**

*Sabarmati Ashram*

## Why is Gujarat's history an illustrious one?

The history of Gujarat goes back to the Indus Valley civilization. The Dravidian tribes were the original inhabitants of the region. Gujarat saw an Aryan invasion, followed by a brief period of Greek rule. Later, there was a succession of Hindu kingdoms, including the era of the Guptas. This era ended in the reign of the Solankis. The 9th century witnessed the emergence of the Muslims in the po-litical arena of the state. The rule of the Mughals lasted for two centuries before the Marathas ended it in the 18th century.

The British Raj came to Gujarat in 1803. After independence, Gujarat was included under the old Bombay state. Bombay was finally divided into two separate states- Gujarat and Maharashtra.

*Surat*

*Sardar Sarovar Project*

### What do we know about the geography of Gujarat?

**G**ujarat is situated on the west coast of India. The state is bound by the Arabian Sea on the west, Pakistan and Rajasthan in the north and northeast, Madhya Pradesh in the southeast, and Maharashtra in the south. It has a very long coastline, extending to more than 1290 kms. Gujarat is made up of three geographical regions. The peninsula, traditionally known as Saurashtra, is essentially a hilly tract sprinkled with low mountains. Kutch, on the northeast is barren and rocky, and includes the famous Rann Desert. The third region extends from the Rann of Kutch and the Aravalli Hills to the River Damanganga. It is on the whole, a level plain of alluvial soil. The forest cover in

*Vadodara*

Tell Me Why

*IIM, Ahmedabad*

We are developing our economy with an Agricultural Industrial Revolution!

Gujarat is relatively little, with only 9.61% area covered with forest. However, it still supports more than 40 species of animals including the rare Asiatic lion, wild ass, and blackbuck. The rivers of the state are mostly seasonal streams, and the highest point in Gujarat is in the Girnar Hills.

**Why is Gujarat's growth impressive?**

Gujarat is one of the most prosperous states of India owing to its agricultural productivity and industrial development. The state leads the country in various industrial sectors namely, textiles, automobiles, engineering, chemicals, petrochemicals, drugs and pharmaceuticals, dairy, cement, ceramics, gems and jewellery. Major agricultural products include cotton, groundnuts, dates, sugar cane, milk and milk products. The world's largest grass root refinery is the oil refinery in Jamnagar. The world's largest ship breaking yard is in Gujarat, and Gujarat is the only state in India to have a statewide gas grid of 2,200kms. Gujarat ranks first in the nation in gas based thermal electricity generation. During the past few years from 1994 to 2011, Gujarat's has had an average growth rate of 12.4 % per annum, which is a very impressive growth rate indeed.

## Why was Gujarat able to become an industrial power?

Gujarat has rich natural resources, a vast reservoir of skilled manpower, and one of the most developed industrial infrastructures in the country. Its rank among the states has steadily risen from 8th in 1960, and it is now vying for the top slot.

From its traditional textile base, Gujarat has diversified into fields like chemicals, petrochemicals, engineering, pharmaceuticals, dyes & dye intermediates, food processing, agro-based industries,

*Ahmedabad*

dairy, edible oils, and a host of other sectors. The policies pursued by the state have resulted in increasing employment opportunities, promoting entrepreneurs belonging to weaker sections, and also in improving the export performance of the state. The state has been able to attract substantial flow of investment to the industrial sector during last couple of decades.

### Garba and Bandini
Gujarat is famous for its garba dance, and bandini work. Garba is a popular folk dance that is associated with Lord Krishna. Bandini is an ancient art that involves tying and dyeing pieces of cotton or silk, with natural colours.

CURIOUS FACT

*Garba Dance*

Tell Me Why

# Haryana

Capital : **Chandigarh**
Districts : **20**
Principal Language : **Hindi**
State Bird : **Black Francolin**
State Animal : **Blackbuck**
State Flower : **Lotus**

## Why does Haryana have a unique place in Indian history?

Haryana has been a cradle of Indian culture and civilization. It was here, 5,000 long years ago that Lord Krishna preached the gospel of duty to Arjuna. The region has been the scene of many a war because of its being 'a gateway to North India'.

As years rolled by, successive streams of the Huns, the Turks and the Tughlaqs invaded India and decisive battles were fought on this land. At the end of the 14th century, Timur led an army through this area to Delhi. Later, the Mughals defeated the Lodhis in the historic battle of Panipat in the year 1526. Towards the middle of the 18th century, the Marathas had established their sway over Haryana. The area was ceded to the British in 1803. In 1832, it was transferred to the then

Welcome to the cradle of wars. Sorry, cradle of Indian civilization.

HARYANA

*Farms of Haryana*

*Maruti Manufacturing Plant at Gurgaon*

North-Western Provinces and in 1858, Haryana became a part of Punjab, remaining as such after the partition of India in 1947.

The demand for Haryana as a separate state, however, was raised even before India's independence in 1947, and Haryana became India's 17th state on 1st November 1966. Haryana was carved out of the mostly Hindi-speaking eastern portion of Punjab, while the mostly Punjabi-speaking western portion remained as current day Punjab. The city of Chandigarh, was made a union territory to serve as capital of both these states.

## What are the highlights of Haryana's geography?

Haryana is small state, bounded by Uttar Pradesh in the east, Punjab in the west, Himachal Pradesh in the north, and Rajasthan in the south. Most of Haryana is in the plains, with the Aravalli mountain range starting its westward journey from here. In addition to the Shivalik Hills, the dry irregular Aravalli Hills and the Gaggar Yamuna Plain, parts of Hary-

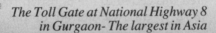

*The Toll Gate at National Highway 8 in Gurgaon- The largest in Asia*

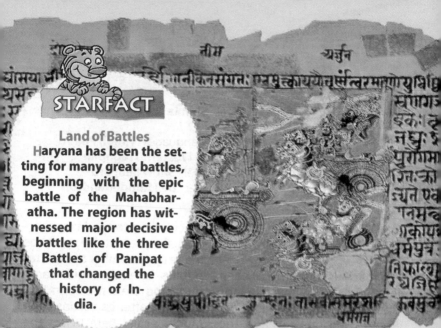

ana are made up of a semi desert sandy plain that borders Rajasthan.

The Yamuna is the only major river that passes through this small state, which is one of the greenest in the country. The ancient river Saraswati was thought to have flows through

*Manuscript Illustration of the Battle of Kurukshetra*

Haryana, but it has now disappeared. The River Ghaggar is its main seasonal river. It rises up in the outer Himalayas between the Yamuna and the Sutlej, and then enters Haryana.

*River Yamuna*

# Himachal Pradesh

Capital : **Shimla**
Districts : **12**
Principal Languages : **Hindi, Pahari**
State Bird : **Western Tragopan**
State Animal : **Snow Leopard**
State Flower : **Bell Rhododendron**

## Why is Himachal Pradesh's history said to be steeped in antiquity?

**H**imachal Pradesh has been inhabited by human beings since the dawn of civilization. About 2 million years ago, the foothills of Himachal Pradesh were inhabited by people from the Indus valley civilization, which flourished between 2250 and 1750 BC. The people of the Indus valley civilization pushed out the original inhabitants, who came and settled in what is now Himachal Pradesh.

According to the Mahabharatha, the present day state was made up of number of small republics. Later, the region came under the rule of the Gupta Empire, and after its collapse, the Mughals ruled here. In fact, the chiefs of the region, and the Mughal rulers had made some joint settlements. Ranjit Singh conquered some parts of the area during the nineteenth century. The Gorkhas were in power for a while until the British subjugated the Gorkha tribe, and conquered some parts of the region. After independence, Himachal Pradesh came into being as a Union Territory when more than 30 princely states were integrated in 1948. Later, in 1966, the hilly areas of

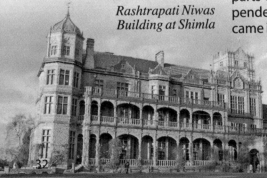

*Rashtrapati Niwas Building at Shimla*

Punjab were merged with the state, increasing its size. Himachal Pradesh became the 18th state of India on 25th January, 1971.

*Dal Lake, Himachal Pradesh*

composed almost entirely of mountains that range from 350 metres to 6,975 metres above sea level. It is a part of the Indian Himalayas, and has wide valleys, imposing snow capped mountains, limpid lakes, rivers, and gushing streams. The state can be divided into three zones. They are the outer Himalayas or the Shivaliks, the inner or the middle Himalayas, and the greater Himalayas or the Alpines. More than half of the state is under thick forest cover. There are around 1200 species of birds and 359 species of animals in Himachal Pradesh. There are several major rivers running through the state, including the Beas River, which flows through the Kullu Valley, the Chenab River in Lahaul, and the Spiti River, which joins the Sutlej River in Kinnaur.

**Why is Shimla a popular tourist destination?**

Shimla, the capital of Himachal Pradesh is a beautiful hill station. It derives its name from 'Goddess Shyamla', who is supposed to be an avatar of Goddess

I have a 5000 year old knife!

**Why is the geography of Himachal Pradesh very interesting?**

The state of Himachal Pradesh has boundaries with Jammu and Kashmir in the North, Uttar Pradesh in the Southeast, China in the east, Haryana in the south, and Punjab in the west. The geography of Himachal Pradesh is very interesting as the state is

*Shimla, Capital of Himachal Pradesh*

*The Kalka-Shimla Railway*

Kali. Shimla was the summer capital of India under the British rule, and is today a popular tourist destination for visitors from other states and abroad.

Shimla is referred to as 'the queen of the hills'. It is draped in forests of pine, rhododendron, and oak, and is surrounded by snow capped peaks. Within the town are a host of splendid colonial edifices, quaint cottages, and charming walks. Among the attractions are the stately Viceregal Lodge, charming iron lamp posts, and Anglo-Saxon names. The Mall, packed with shops and eateries, is the centre of attraction of the town, and Scandal Point offers a view of distant snow clad peaks. The snowfall during the winters attracts many tour-

*Khajjiar Hill Station, Himachal Pradesh*

ists, and Shimla then becomes home to winter-sports, and an ice-skating carnival. Now, don't you feel like visiting Shimla too?

Tell Me Why

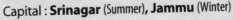

# Jammu and Kashmir

Capital : **Srinagar** (Summer), **Jammu** (Winter)
Districts : **22**
Principal Languages : **Urdu, Kashmiri, Dogri**
State Bird : **Black-necked Crane**
State Animal : **Kashmir stag**
State Flower : **Lotus**

*Dal Lake, Srinagar*

## How was Jammu and Kashmir formed?

In the history of Jammu and Kashmir, the Maurya dynasty took control of the region around the 3rd BC. King Ashoka ruled the land for a considerable period of time, and Buddhism was widely practiced. During the time of the Mughals, Islam was widely practiced, and Akbar had a strong influence in the region for many years.

Later, the control of the Kashmir valley was passed to the conquering Sikh armies. Gulab Singh was made the Raja of Jammu in 1820.

In 1846, Jammu and Kashmir came into existence as a united state. After independence, Maharaja Hari Singh, the ruler of Jammu and Kashmir was given the freedom to opt to become a part of either India or Pakistan. In October 1947 the Pasthuns from Pakistan invaded the Kashmir valley, and the Raja sought assistance from India. In return for India's help, the Raja signed the Instrument of Accession, making Jammu and Kashmir a part of India.

*Ladakh*

**Tulip Park**

The Indira Gandhi Tulip Park in Srinagar is the largest of its kind in Asia. The tulips cover an area of over 12 acres, and the garden remains in full bloom for a month. Row upon row of tulip beds, 50 metres long and 2.5 m wide, stretch far into the horizon. Pink, yellow, and red tulips are followed by blooms in all colours imaginable- even black! It is truly a breath taking sight.

## What do we know about Jammu and Kashmir?

Jammu and Kashmir is the northernmost state of the Indian union. It is bounded by Afghanistan, Pakistan, and China. The state can be divided into three regions- Jammu, the Kashmir Valley, and Ladakh. It has two capitals- Jammu, the winter capital, and Srinagar, the summer capital.

Jammu and Kashmir is famous for its natural beauty, and has been described as 'heaven on earth'. Tourism is a very important industry here, and some major attractions are Gulmarg, Pahalgam, Leh, Patnitop, and Ladakh. The city of Jammu is known as the city of temples, while Srinagar is famous for its lakes and houseboats, and Kashmir is known for its magnificent scenery. In fact, the

Is it winter or summer...? I want to go to Kashmir.

*Kargil*

*Poonch*

## What are the geographical features of Jammu and Kashmir?

The state of Jammu and Kashmir is mainly hilly and mountainous, with valleys and stretches of plains. The area is full of natural beauty with thick forests, fast flowing rivers and winding streams. The main rivers are Jhelum, Neelum, and Poonch. The state can be divided into four major regions. They are the sub-mountainous and semi-mountainous plain known as kandi or dry belt, the Shivalik ranges, the high mountainous zone, and the middle run of the Indus River.

In Jammu, the flora ranges from the thorny bushes type of the arid plain to the temperate and alpine flora of the higher altitudes. Kashmir is also resplendent with forests. The most magnificent of the Kashmir trees is the chinar. The mountain ranges in the valley have dense deodar, pine, and fir. The highest elevations have no vegetation- just snow and ice.

Kashmir Valley is surrounded by some of the highest mountain ranges in the world. The two most important pilgrimage centers are the Amarnath Caves, and the Vaishnodevi Shrine.

Agriculture is the most important occupation of the people here. Even those engaged in other industries depend on agriculture for raw material. Most of the people follow Islam, Hinduism and Buddhism.

# Jharkhand

Capital : **Ranchi**
Districts : **22**
Principal Language : **Hindi**
State Bird : **Asian Koel**
State Animal : **Indian Elephant**
State Flower : **Parrot Tree**

## Why was Jharkhand formed as a separate state?

The state of Jharkhand existed, and was distinct in its identity from ancient times. Raja Jai Singh Deo of Orissa was accepted as the ruler of Jharkhand by its people in the 13th century. The local tribal heads had developed into barbaric dictators, and so, the people of this state approached the more powerful rulers of the neighbouring state hoping to be ruled more justly. This became the turning point in the history of the region.

During the Mughal period, the Jharkhand area was known as Kukara. After the year 1765, it came under the control of the British Empire, and became formally known under its present title, 'Jharkhand' - the land of jungles and jharis or bushes.

*Tatanagar Railway Station*

STARFACT

### Bokaro Steel Plant

The Bokaro Steel Plant in Jharkhand, is the largest steel mill in Asia. It is part of Bokaro Steel City, one of the most important industrial cities in India. The city is well planned, and famous for its excellent education system.

Tell Me Why

However, the adivasis of Jharkhand began what would become a series of repeated revolts against British colonial rule. When India became independent, Jharkhand was a part of Bihar.

The Jharkhand Mukti Morcha started a movement for a separate state, which caught the interest of a large section of the people of this area, and eventually emerged into a political agitation. In Au-

*A Coal mine in Dhanbad*

gust 2000, the Parliament of India passed the Bihar Reorganization Bill, which carved 18 districts out of Bihar to form Jharkhand state. On 15th November 2000, Jharkhand became the 28th state of India.

States of India

## Why is Jharkhand called 'The land of forests'?

**A**lmost one third of Jharkhand is covered by forests. Most of the forests of Jharkhand were privately owned until the zamindari system was abolished under the Bihar Land Reforms Act, 1950. These evergreen forests abound with wildlife sanctuaries, lakes, and waterfalls. They are also a source of many forest products that are of great economic value to the state. Jharkhand is also blessed with natural resources such as copper, coal, iron, manganese, mica, chromite, and bauxite. Although Jharkhand is endowed with vast and rich natural resources, mainly minerals and forests, 80 per cent of its population depends mainly on agriculture and allied activities for a living.

*Sita Falls, Ranchi*

The Ganges, the Damodar, the Mayurakshi, the Barakar, the Koel, the Sankh, the Sone, the Auranga, the Kharkai, the Swarnarekha, the Gumani and the Batane are the rivers that nourish this land. Most of the Jharkhand region is part of the Chota Nagpur plateau and Parasnath Hill, at a height of 1365.5 metres, is the highest peak of the state. It is a major Jain pilgrimage centre.

*Birla Institute of Technology*

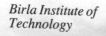

## Why is the culture of Jharkhand a triumph of the tribal spirit?

The culture of Jharkhand has been shaped by the tribal communities that abound in this region. The oldest cave paintings in India are believed to have been the work of a Jharkhand tribe called the Shabars. When the tribes of Jharkhand gather to celebrate a special occasion, the music and dance are a reflection of the rhythm of their lives. Many types of percussion instruments are popular, especially the nagara. Dance forms echo the warrior like movements of battles fought long ago. Some of the most famous dances of the region are the Paika and the Chhau. The different crafts of Jharkhand, which form an important part of the people's lives, culture and festivals include wood crafts, bamboo crafts, Paitkar paintings and metal works.

# Karnataka

Capital : **Bengaluru**
Districts : **27**
Principal Language : **Kannada**
State Bird : **Indian Roller**
State Animal : **Indian Elephant**
State Flower : **Lotus**

## How was Karnataka formed?

**W**e know that the Mauryas ruled over the major part of what is now Karnataka in the third century BC. After the Mauryas, the Satavahanas ruled Karnataka for nearly 300 years. They were followed by a series of dynasties including the Kadambas, the Gangas and the Pallavas.

After the 13th century, the Vijayanagar Empire flourished. This was a period of great wealth and prosperity for the region. However, the Vijayanagar Empire started to decline by the end of the 16th century, and the Mughuls then dominated the region until the British took control in 1799. When India became independent, Karnataka was known as Mysore State. There was some reorganization of territories in 1953 and 1956, and ultimately, modern Karnataka came into existence as a state of the Indian Union in 1973.

*Vidhana Soudha- State Legislative Assembly*

Oh! But I want to go to Karnataka state!

MYSORE STATE

### Why is Karnataka called a land of geographical diversity?

**K**arnataka is the eighth largest state in India. It is situated on the western edge of the Deccan plateau, and is surrounded by Maharashtra and Goa on the north, Andhra Pradesh on the east, and Tamil Nadu and Kerala on the south. On the west, it opens out on the Arabian Sea. Karnataka occupies three natural regions like the Coastal Strip, the Sahyadris, and the Deccan Plateau. They are known in Kannada as Paschima Karavali,

*River Kaveri*

Malnad and Maidan respectively.

Karnataka has chains of mountains, the highest being the Mullayyana Giri. The Sahyadri is covered with evergreen forests. They drop abruptly towards the Arabian Sea, thus forming a natural barrier between the plateau and the coastal regions. The plateau region is drained by the two principal rivers namely the Krishna, and the Kaveri. The average elevation of the plateau is about 610 metres above sea-level. With mountains, plateaus, and a lush coastal region, Karnataka

*Yakshagana*

42

national airport. Greenfield airports are those that are built from scratch in a new location. Bengaluru International Airport is surrounded by some of the most eco-friendly settlements, and no development will be allowed on the natural river valleys in the area.

is indeed a land of great geographical diversity.

**Why are Bengaluru and Mysore important cities in Karnataka?**

Bengaluru ( Bangalore) is the fifth largest city in India. It is located 1000 metres above sea level, and has a refreshing climate. Bengaluru is a perfect blend of natural beauty, man made marvels, and technology. It is often called the Silicon Valley of India, because of the large number of software companies that have set up shop and operate out of state-of-the-art facilities. Bengaluru plays host to international-class conferences, workshops and exhibitions devoted to the software cause.

Mysore is often called the city of palaces. It was the capital of the former rulers of Mysore State, and contains many architectural gems. Mysore is the second largest city in the state of Karnataka, and is famous for the festivities that take place during the Dassera festival held every year. Besides its numerous palaces and royal buildings, Mysore City is also known for proximity to several other places of interest such as Srirangapatna, Krishnaraja Sagar Dam and Shivanasamudra Falls. In addition to its many attractions, Mysore City is also known for its sandalwood products.

*Indian Institute of Science*

States of India

## Why is Karnataka a cultural treasure house?

Karnataka has a distinct culture that reflects its glorious past and vibrant present. In dance, art, sculpture, literature and classical music, Karnataka leads the way. It has the oldest literary tradition among the Dravidian languages. Evidence of this is found in the 9th century treatise on poetry called the 'Kavirajamarga', where references are made to earlier writings. The three 'gems of Kannada literature' are the poets Pampa, Ponna and Ranna. They lived during the 10th and 12th centuries.

Carnatic music is different from that of Hindustani music. The stringed tanpura, the mridangam, the ghatam and violins usually accompany a vocal music recital. Karnataka has a particularly rich culture of folk theatre. The most famous forms are Yakshagana, which features a single narrator, and Bayalata, which has multiple narrative voices. The lesser-known forms are the Dasarata and Sannata, and the Dodatta. A very famous craft of Karnataka is bidriware. Originally produced in the town of Bidar, this metal craft is made by inlaying silver or gold in blackened metal. Is it any wonder then that Karnataka is considered to be a cultural treasure house?

Sa.. ree... ga...ma...

# Kerala

Capital : **Thiruvananthapuram**
Districts : **14**
Principal Language : **Malayalam**
State Bird : **Great Hornbill**
State Animal : **Indian Elephant**
State Flower : **Golden Shower Tree**

*Boat Race in Kerala*

**Why has Kerala's geographical position given it an identity of its own?**

Kerala is a small state situated on the south west coast of India. It is only around 550 kms long and 120 kms wide, and is bordered by land on three sides and by the Arabian Sea on the west. Kerala shares its borders with Karnataka in the north and northeast, and with Tamil Nadu in the east and south. Its geographical position between the Arabian Sea and the Western Ghats has protected it from invaders, and given it a distinct identity of its own.

Kerala is divided into three geographical regions- the highlands, the midlands, and the coastal areas. The highlands slope down from the Western Ghats. This is the area of

This is 'kera' from Kerala.

*Kerala Legislative Assembly*

major plantations like tea, coffee, rubber, and various spices. The midlands lie between the mountains and the lowlands, and are made up of undulating hills and valleys. This is an area of intensive cultivation. Cashew, coconut, arecanut, tapioca, banana and vegetables of different varieties are grown in this area. The coastal area is made up of numerous shallow lagoons, river deltas, backwaters, and the shores of the Arabian Sea.

Even though Kerala is a small state, 44 rivers water the land, of which 41 are west flowing, and 3 flow eastward. Kerala is also bestowed with a number of lakes and backwater lagoons which add to the beauty of the land.

*Coconut Trees in Kerala*

## Why is the history of Kerala so interesting?

The history of Kerala goes back to ancient times, and much of it is cloaked in myths and legends. What is known though, is that trade flourished here as early as 3000 BC. In fact, Muziris, also known as Kodungalloor or Cranganore, was reputed to be the ancient world's greatest trading centre in the east. Around the first century AD, Jewish immigrants arrived here, and St. Thomas the Apostle also brought Christianity to these shores around that time. Later, Islam was brought to Kerala by Arab traders, between the 6th and 8th centuries AD.

Till around the 5th century AD, Kerala was controlled by the eastern Pandya, Chola, and Chera dynasties. The period between 800 AD and 1100 AD is

Tell Me Why

known as the period of 'Second Chera' Empire. With the breakdown of the Chera Empire, the next phase of Kerala history began. This was the period of the provincial rulers. These provinces were once part of the Chera Empire. The provincial rulers were confined to small areas, but they frequently fought each other for domination.

The Portuguese arrived in 1498, and dominated trade in the region until the arrival of the Dutch, in the 17th century. King Marthanda Varma of the kingdom of Travancore defeated the Dutch and expanded the boundaries of his kingdom. However, by 1806, both Travancore and Cochin became subject states under British control. At the time of India's independence in 1947, there were three separate territories in the region that is now Kerala. They were Malabar, Cochin, and Travancore. In 1949, Cochin and Travancore merged, and later, Malabar was added, and the new state of Kerala was born on November 1st 1956.

Where can we meet God in this God's own country?

*Kovalam Beach*

**STARFACT**

## Kathakali

Kathakali, one of the oldest forms of theatre, is a blend of dance, music and acting. It dramatizes stories, which are mostly adapted from the Indian epics. The dancer expresses himself through hand gestures and facial expressions. Kathakali means 'story-play,' and this dance form, full of vigour and passion, also known as the 'king of the performing arts,' in India.

## Why is Kerala called God's own country?

Kerala is known as 'God's own country' for its stunning natural beauty, pleasant climate, unique culture, and its streamlined infrastructure. The phrase was coined in the 1980's to launch a tourism initiative that was so successful that it transformed the state from a relatively unknown tourist destination into one of the most preferred holiday destinations in the world! From sun kissed beaches to cloud shrouded peaks, from wild life sanctuaries to breath taking festivals- Kerala has it all in the blessed abundance that makes it truly God's own country.

## Why is Kerala's culture considered a blend of the best of different cultures?

Kerala takes pride in its rich cultural heritage. It has a precious legacy handed down by different races, religions, and communities, and it represents the collective achievement of the people in the fields of music and dance, religion and philosophy, language and literature, art, and architecture. Kathakali is a 300 year old dance form that combines

*Great Hornbill*

the elements of opera, ballet, masque and pantomime. Some of the other unique dance forms are Krishnanattom, Koodiyattom, Mohiniyattom, Thullal, Oppana and Chavittunatakam.

The traditional music of Kerala is Sopanam, which is also used as a background score during Kathakali performances. The influence of Carnatic music started from the 19th century, when the King of Travancore, Swathi Thirunal Rama Varma popularized it. Other than Sopanam, Melam is widely performed in the temples across the state during the temple festivals.

Kerala is renowned for its carvings in rosewood and sandalwood. The state boasts

*Mohiniyattam*

of an abounding tradition of artists. Who has not heard of the great painter Raja Ravi Varma? The traditional Kerala murals display a distinct style and colour code dominated by ochres and greens. The festivals celebrated with dance, music and passion are also a sign of the culture. Onam is one of the major festivals of the state, and a time for thanksgiving with sumptuous feasts, boat races, and other sports.

*Thrissur Pooram*

# Madhya Pradesh

Capital : **Bhopal**
Districts : **50**
Principal Language : **Hindi**
State Bird : **Asian Paradise Flycatcher**
State Animal : **Barasingha**
State Flower : **Parrot Tree**

*Khajuraho*

## Which is the second largest state in India?

**M**adhya Pradesh, the second largest state in the nation, lies in the centre of India. It shares its borders with seven neighbouring states. They are Rajasthan and Uttar Pradesh, Maharashtra and Gujarat, Andhra Pradesh, Chhattisgarh and Jharkhand. Forests cover a major part of Madhya Pradesh, and the cultivated area amounts to almost half of the total area. The state covers a wide area of the Indian plateau region. The Chambal, Sone, Betwa, and other rivers flow from the west to the east. The basins of these rivers divide this state into two parts. The northern part drains into the Ganges, while the southern part drains into the river systems of the Mahanadi and the Godavari rivers.

## Why do we say that the history of Madhya Pradesh is one of kingdoms and empires?

Madhya Pradesh has been home to many empires and these include the Mauryan Empire, the Mughals and later,

*Vidhan Sabha, Madhya Pradesh*

**Sanchi Stupas**
The Emperor Asoka built many stupas in honour of Lord Buddha. Stupas are towering stone structures in which the relics of Buddha were placed. The stupas at Sanchi, a small village in Madhya Pradesh, are re-

*Sanchi Stupa*

by the British. This is a land of empires and kingdoms, of great warriors and builders, poets and musicians, saints and philosophers. Hinduism, Islam, Buddhism and Jainism were all nurtured and flourished here. Dynasties like that of Sungas, Andhras, Satavahanas, Ksaptrapas, Nagas and the Guptas ruled over this land. During, and after the 10th century, different regions of the state were ruled by different dynasties.

When the British took over, the state was declared as the Central Province. After India gained her independence, Madhya Pradesh was given the status of a full-fledged state with effect from 1st November 1956.

markable in that they trace the development of Buddhist architecture and sculpture from the 3rd century to the 12th century.

States of India

51

**Why is the culture of Madhya Pradesh called a melting pot of different cultures?**

Madhya Pradesh has been home to Hindus, Jains, Buddhists, Muslims, and various tribes, and all of them have left an indelible mark in the form of temples, stupas, palaces and singer in Akbar's court. The region saw the rise of two major gharanas of music that were born and nurtured here. Just like the music of the region, the dance of this state is equally unique and varied. Dominated by the tribal populace, the folk dance of the state is tribal in na-

*Bansagar Dam*

*Forest in Madhya Pradesh*

other architectural land marks. This is why the state is called a melting pot of different cultures.

Madhya Pradesh has a rich history in music. This land saw the birth of two great singers of history– Tansen and Baiju Bawra. Baiju Bawra created a niche for himself in Persian, and sung in the Mughal king Humayun's court, while Tansen who succeeded him, became a ture. Madhya Pradesh is host to the world famous Khajuraho Dance Festival. Masters of different dances like Kuchipudi, Bharatnatyam, Odissi, Kathak and many other classical dances perform here with the backdrop of floodlit Khajuraho temples. Besides these dances, a folk theatre called Macch showcases the legends of kings and warriors through traditional songs and dances.

52

## Why do we say that rivers play an important role in Madhya Pradesh?

Madhya Pradesh lies at the heart of India, and boasts of ten river basins. The Narmada and Tapti Rivers, and their basins divide the state in two. The northern part drains into the Ganga basin, and the southern part into the Godavari and Mahanadi systems. The Chambal, Sone, Betwa, Mahanadi and Indravati rivers flow from the western side of the state to the east, while Narmada and Tapti flows from the eastern side to the west. A major tributary of the Ganga, the Son, is born in this state, as are the Narmada and Mahanadi Rivers.

*Bhil Tribal Girls*

The Narmada, Chambal, Betwa, Shipra, Sone, Mahanadi, Indrawati and Tapti are all rivers have played a considerable role in making Madhya Pradesh what it is today. In fact, the Narmada is also referred to as the lifeline of Madhya Pradesh. Originating in Amarkantak, the highest peak of the Vindhya Range, it flows westward through Madhya Pradesh and Gujarat before finally ending its journey in the Gulf of Khambat.

*Godavari*

Where is Madhya Pradesh..?

# Maharashtra

Capital : **Mumbai**
Districts : **35**
Principal Language : **Marathi**
State Bird : **Green Imperial Pigeon**
State Animal : **Indian Giant Squirrel**
State Flower : **Jarul**

*Pune*

## What do we know about the birth of Maharashtra?

**T**he name Maharashtra first appeared in a 7th century inscription and may have originated from the word rathi, meaning 'chariot driver'. It probably refers to the builders and drivers of chariots who formed the maharathis, or a 'fighting force'. The word 'Maharashtra' also means 'great nation'. The region was first ruled by the hindus, and later by muslims.

Shivaji Bhosle, founder of the Maratha Empire, was born in 1627. At the age of 16, he took an oath to make the land free of the Mughals. This was the start of his lifelong struggle against the Mughals and other Muslim powers. By 1673, he had control over most of western Maharashtra, and was ceremoniously crowned as a sovereign king in 1673. At the time of independence in 1947, the state of Bombay was born. In 1960, Bombay state was divided into two states on the basis of language, with Gujarat in the north, and Maharashtra in the south.

54

Hey... I am making a map of Maharashtra.

## Why is the Sahyadri known as the backbone of Maharashtra?

Maharashtra is the third largest state in the country. The Sahyadri Range forms the backbone of the state. This range has an average height of 1000m, and falls in steep cliffs, to the Konkan on the west. Eastwards, the hill country falls in steps through a transitional area to the plateau level. The Konkan, lying between the Arabian Sea and the Sahyadri Range, is a narrow coastal lowland. The Satpudas, hills along the northern border, and the Bhamragad-Chiroli-Gaikhuri Ranges on the eastern border, form physical barriers preventing easy movement, but also serve as natural limits to the state.

### Festivals of Maharashtra

Maharashtra is a state where all religions co-exist in peaceful harmony, and so, all the main festivals like Holi, Christmas, Diwali and Eid are celebrated joyously. There are also several regional festivals like the Pune Festival, Ganesh Chaturthi, the Elephanta Festival, and Ellora Festival. However, the biggest festival of Maharashtra is undoubtedly Ganesh Chaturthi. It is celebrated between August and September, and lasts for 8 to 10 days. Idols of Lord Ganesh are worshipped, and the end is marked by the spectacular procession that culminates at the Arabian Sea, where the idols are immersed in the water.

*Nariman Point*

*Ajanta Caves*

## Why are the Ajanta and Ellora caves a tribute to ancient Indian art?

Located near the city of Aurangabad in Maharashtra, the Ajanta and Ellora caves are world famous for the cave shrines that are cut out of rock, all by hand. There are 34 caves at Ellora, and 29 caves at Ajanta, and all are outstanding specimens of Indian architectural excellence. They were built using simple tools, and contain some of the most divine sculptures and images of Buddha's preaching. The Ajanta caves lie deep in the semi-arid Sahayadri hills, above the Waghora River. About 30 kms northwest of Aurangabad, the 34 Ellora caves are carved into the sides of a hill.

*Ellora Caves*

**CURIOUS FACT**

### Rivers of Maharashtra

The main rivers of Maharashtra are the Godavari, the Krishna, and the Tapti. The Godavari and Krishna flow eastwards into the Bay of Bengal, irrigating most of central and eastern Maharashtra. To the north, the rivers Tapi and Narmada flow into the Arabian Sea. To the east, are major rivers like Wainganga that flow to the south.

*Mumbai*

**Powerhouse**

Maharashtra is the industrial power-house of India, with a contribution of 13% towards the national economy. Chemical and allied products, electrical and non-electrical machinery, textiles, petroleum and allied products are the main industries in Maharashtra.

*Chhatrapati Shivaji Airport*

city is the home to India's two largest stock markets, the Bombay Stock Exchange, and the National Stock Exchange. It is the financial heart of India, one of the world's top 10 commercial centres, and the entertainment capital of the nation. People flock to the city in droves, for Mumbai is truly the city of golden opportunities.

**Why is Mumbai one of the most important cities in India?**

The present day dynamic and vibrant city of Mumbai was originally an archipelago of seven small islands. In the 3rd century BC, these islands came under Maurya Empire ruled by Emperor Asoka.

After independence, Mumbai has been one of the most progressive cities. It is recognized as the seat of domestic and international trade. The

# Manipur

Capital : **Imphal**
Districts : **9**
Principal Language : **Manipuri**
State Bird : **Mrs. Hume's Pheasant**
State Animal : **Sangai**
State Flower : **Siroi Lily**

## What do we know of Manipur's history?

The history of the region of Manipur goes back to the 1st century AD. It was a kingdom formed by the unification of ten clans. Its modern history started in 1819 AD, when King Marjeet ruled over Manipur. The Burmese defeated him, and Chahi-Taret Khuntakpa became the king. In 1825, Gambir Singh led the Manipuris in an attack over the Burmese, and declared himself as the ruler. The British conquered Manipur on 27th April, 1891 AD. Maharaja Churachand Singh was named as raja and the administration was conducted under British supervision for some years. After India became independent on August 15th, 1947, the Manipur Constitution Act established a democratic form of government, with the Maharaja as the executive head, and a legislature constituted by election on adult franchise. In 1949, Manipur merged with independent India and on 21st January 1972, Manipur was granted statehood.

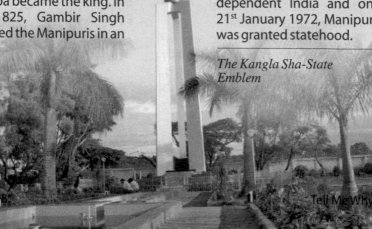

*The Kangla Sha-State Emblem*

Tell Me Why

## Why is Manipur called the 'land of jewels'?

Manipur boasts of an exotic landscape with gently undulating hills, emerald green valleys, blue lakes, and dense forests. Manipur means the land of jewels, and it is well named because Mother Nature has been extra generous in her beauty in this land. Nagaland, Mizoram, Assam and Burma geographically border the present state of Manipur. About 90% of the land is mountainous, and its major river is known as Imphal, after which the capital city was named. Manipur is famous for its orchids and also for its rare and beautiful, and exquisite handicrafts. Its culture is a fine blend of colourful festivals, rich history, vibrant customs, wonderful architecture, enchanting music, and exciting dance forms. The favourite sport of the people of Manipur is archery.

> I am from the land of jewels.

*Dzukou Valley*

*Ras Lila*

*Mukna-*
*A Manipuri Sport*

**Why are festivals an important part of life in Manipur?**

Festivals form an important part of Manipuri life- in fact, hardly a month passes by without a festival of some kind being celebrated. These festivals project the cultural, social and religious aspirations of the people. There is the festival of Laiharaboa that represents the worship of traditional deities and ancestors. Yaoshang is the most important Hindu festival in Manipur. It is a five-day long festival which begins on a full moon day in the month of Phalgun, that is, February and March. Kut is an autumn festival of Kuki-Chin-Mizo group of Manipuri tribes. This festival celebrates the boun-tiful food stock, and is a thanksgiving ceremony.

Other festivals include Ningol Chakouba, which is one of the major festivals in Manipur. It is a social festival where the women are invited to a feast at their parental house. Holi is another major festival of Manipur, and is celebrated for five days starting from the full moon of Phalguna. Gang Ngai is a festival of the Kabui Nagas. It begins with an oath taking ceremony and lasts for five days. Cheiraoba celebrates the Manipuri New Year. During this time of the year, the people clean their houses, decorate them, and start everything afresh. The celebration of this festival includes climbing the nearest hill in with the belief that such an act would help a person to conquer new heights in real life.

*Hiyang Tanaba*

Tell Me Why

# Meghalaya

Capital : **Shillong**
Districts : **7**
Principal Languages : **Khasi, Garo, English**
State Bird : **Hill Myna**
State Animal : **Clouded Leopard**
State Flower : **Lady's Slipper Orchid**

*A Lake in Meghalaya*

## CURIOUS FACT

**Longest Span Cantilever Bridge**

**The Jadukata Bridge is the longest span cantilever bridge in India. The bridge has a central span of 140 metres, and stretches across the Jadulata River, about 130 kms away from Shillong, the capital of Meghalaya. It forms a vital link on an important road in this border state.**

## How was Meghalaya formed?

Meghalaya was once ruled by the ancient tribes known as the Khasis, Jaintias and Garos. Each had its own kingdom. In the 19th century, these kingdoms came under the administration of the British and during the British Raj, Meghalaya was annexed under the British Empire. Further in 1935, Meghalaya became a part of Assam. However, Megha-

I am off to Meghalaya!

## STARFACT

### Mawsynram

The cave of Mawsynram in Meghalaya is a popular tourist destination across India as well as the entire world. It is famous for the gigantic formation of a stalagmite, which resembles the shape of a 'Shivalinga'. The area also holds the record for being the wettest place on Earth with an annual rainfall of 11,873 millimetres.

## Why is Meghalaya called the land of clouds?

Carved out of the former state of Assam, Meghalaya is one of the seven sister states of the North Eastern region, bordered by Assam in the north, and Bangladesh in the south. It is geographically known as the 'Meghalaya Plateau,' or the 'Shillong Plateau'. The area is made of the oldest rock-formations. Meghalaya consists of the Garo, Khasi, and Jaintia Hills, along with the Assam ranges. The Meghalaya Plateau's elevation varies between 150 metres to 1961 metres above sea level. The Plateau is highly dissected, and has an irregular terrain in the western and northern side.

laya enjoyed a semi-independent status due to the treaty that was signed between Meghalaya and the British Crown. When India became independent, the region was included in the state of Assam for administrative reasons. This led to an agitation by the local population. The region was accorded full statehood on January 21st, 1972.

*A Golf Course*

Rivers form an important part of the geography of Meghalaya. In the Garo Hills, the major rivers are the Ringgi, Kalu, Ajagar, Sanda, Daring, and Simsan. In the eastern and central parts of the Meghalaya Plateau, the major rivers are the Digaru, Umkhri, Kynchiang and Myntdu. The word Meghalaya means the 'land of clouds' in Sanskrit, and the name is most appropriate for this land of hills and plateaus that seem to touch the clouds.

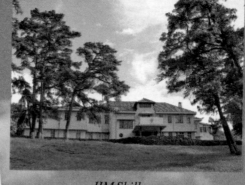
*IIM Shillong*

*A Water Fall*

**CURIOUS FACT**

**Tourism in Meghalaya**

**M**eghalaya is a tourist's paradise and is home to some of the most pristine forests in India. With its many national parks, deep valleys, arching waterfalls, and charming villages, it is a great getaway destination indeed. The second wettest place on Earth, Cherrapunjee, is in Meghalaya. It gets over 11,430 millimetres of rain every year, inundating virtually the entire area for months at a time and tourists flock here for the experience.

# Mizoram

Capital : **Aizawl**
Districts : **8**
Principal Languages : **Mizo, English**
State Bird : **Mrs. Hume's Pheasant**
State Animal : **Hoolock Gibbon**
State Flower : **Red Vanda**

*Aizawl, Mizoram*

## Why was the Mizo National Front formed?

**N**ot much of Mizoram's early history is recorded. It is believed that the Mizos migrated to this region hundreds of years ago. The earliest Mizos who mi-grated to India were known as Kukis. During the period 1750-1850, migrations led to settlements in the hills. The tribal groups were governed under a hereditary chieftainship. Mizoram became a part of the territory of British India in 1891, though the administration of the villages was left to the local chieftains. After India became independent, Mizoram continued to be part of Assam. In 1961, the Mizo National Front was formed with the goal of achieving independence for Greater Mizoram. As a result, the district was carved out of Assam, and raised to the status of a union territory on January 21, 1972. In 1987, Mizoram became the 23rd full-fledged state of the country.

Look at My Mizo orchids!

Tell Me Why

**I**n the pre-British days, Mizo youths over the age of 15 had to stay in bachelor's dormitories, known as Zawlbuk where they received training in tribal welfare wrestling, hunting, and village government. The boys who went to the Zawlbuk emerged as complete men. The training was intensive and strenuous, and strict discipline was maintained in these dormitories.

## Why is Mizoram considered to be a beautiful state?

**M**izoram, a state situated on the extreme south of North-Eastern India, is a land of unending natural beauty. It is a land of hills, the highest being Blue Mountain at 2165 metres. The hills here are covered with bamboo and banana trees, along with a wonderful array of pine trees. The forests in this region also house some of the rarest varieties of orchids,

*A Landscape-Mizoram*

found only in this region of the country. The presence of some major rivers like Tlau, Tlawng, Tuirini, Serlui and Mat and some picturesque lakes is also a highpoint of Mizoram's beauty.

## What are the traditional dances of Mizoram?

**T**he dances of Mizoram get their inspiration from the natural beauty of the hilly terrains. The Khuallam dance of Mizoram is known as the dance of the guests. Males wearing a traditional costume called Puandum perform it. Both males and females perform the Cheraw

*Bamboo Dance*

dance. The use of bamboo staves is a unique trait of this dance. Sarlamkai, is an ancient dance that was performed by the warriors of yore. Boys and girls perform Chheihlam dance using bamboo tubes and drums. Zangtalam is another fascinating dance that is accompanied by deft drummers. Did you know that when a wife dies, the husband performs the dance of Chawnglaizawn?

**Dampa Tiger Reserve**
**The Dampa Tiger Reserve, the biggest wildlife sanctuary in Mizoram, is situated in the western part of Mizoram state on the international border with Bangladesh. It has a variety of rare and endangered animals in abundance, including of course, tigers! Here, evergreen and deciduous forests are found, along with steep precipitous hills, deep valleys, jungle streams, rippling rivulets and natural salts licks.**

This is a special dance item...

Tell Me Why

# Nagaland

Capital : **Kohima**     Districts : **8**

Principal Languages : **English, Angami, Ao, Chang, Konyak, Lotha, Sangtam, Sema and Chakhesang**

State Bird : **Blyth's Tragopan**

State Animal : **Mithun**

State Flower: **Rhododendron**

## Why was Nagaland formed?

**W**e know very little about the early history of Nagaland. During the early 19<sup>th</sup> century, present day Nagaland was under the control of Myanmar. When the British East India Company took over Assam, Nagaland became a part of British India.

After India got her independence in 1947, the area under Nagaland and Assam were combined to form a single state, known as Assam. But as demand for a separate political entity from the Naga tribes intensified, the Government of India decided to make Nagaland a single administrative unit. It became a union territory in 1957, and was governed directly by the centre. How-

*Mithun*

ever, this did not satisfy the Naga tribes. They wanted their own state.

Finally, on 1<sup>st</sup> December 1963, Nagaland became the 16<sup>th</sup> state of India.

## What do we know about the geography of Nagaland?

**N**agaland is located on the extreme north east, just below Arunachal Pradesh. The terrain is hilly, rugged, and mountainous. The highest peak is Saramati in the Twensang district, which is 3840 metres above sea level. The average height of the peaks is between 900 and 1200 metres. The hillsides are covered with green forests. In fact, 20 percent of the total land area of the state is covered with wooded forest, rich in flora and fauna. The only well known lake is Lacham.

The state of Nagaland is drained by four chief rivers of Doyang, Jhanji, Dhansiri and Dikhu. The rivers are the tributaries of the mighty Brahmaputra River, with their sources in the mountain ranges of the state.

*Blyth's Tragopan*

## Why do we say that Nagaland has a rich cultural heritage?

**T**he people of Nagaland are divided into several tribes. The social structure of each and every Naga tribe is different from the other. The Naga tribes still perform their war dances, that are resplendent with colourful and traditional headdresses, costumes, war paint, and weapons like spears. Weaving is a traditional craft passed down the genera-

**In Harmony with the Environment**

For centuries, the Naga tribes have lived in harmony with their environment. They have always been self sufficient, producing their own food, clothing, and shelter. Their culture and lifestyle show their deep respect for Nature.

● *Aravind Bhat*

*Terrace Cultivation in Nagaland*

tions. Almost every rural home has a loom. Naga shawls have their own clan motifs and are brightly coloured. The tribal men make decorative spears and bamboo shields. They are excellent woodcarvers. Basket making is another craft at which the Nagas are skilled. The traditional ornaments of Nagaland also reflect the rich cultural heritage of the people.

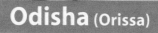

## Odisha (Orissa)

Capital : **Bhubaneshwar**
Districts : **30**
Principal Languages : **Oriya**
State Bird : **Male Indian Peafowl**
State Animal : **Indian Elephant**
State Flower : **Lotus**

*Konark Sun Temple Chariot Wheel*

**Why did the Kalinga war have a great impact on the history of Odisha?**

In ancient times, Odisha was known as Utkala, Kalinga and Odra Desa at different points in its history. For many centuries, Kalinga was a very powerful kingdom. The famous war that the Emperor Asoka waged against Kalinga proved to be a turning point in his life. The bloodshed and killing of war sickened him, and led him to renounce violence, and turn to Buddhism.

This war had a great impact on the history of this region too, for under Asoka's benevolent guidance, literature, language, music, and dance flourished here during ancient times. In 1568, the last Hindu ruler was over-thrown by a Muslim general, and finally, Odisha was annexed by Akbar in 1592. The Mughals ruled till 1803, when Odisha came into British possession. Following India's independence, the 26 princely states in the region were merged into modern state of Odisha.

70

## What do we know about the geography of Odisha?

**O**disha lies on the eastern coast of India. It is bounded by West Bengal in northeast, Jharkhand in the north, Madhya Pradesh in the west, Andhra Pradesh in the south, and the Bay of Bengal in the east. Orissa can be divided into three broad regions - the coastal plains, the middle mountainous country and the plateaus. The region of the coastal plains is a combination of several deltas formed by the major rivers of Odisha, such as the Subarnarekha, the Budhabalanga, the Baitarani, the Brahmani, the Mahanadi, and the Rushikulya. The middle mountainous region covers about three-fourths of the entire state and comprises the hills and mountains of the Eastern Ghats. The plateaus are mostly eroded tablelands, forming the western slopes of the Eastern Ghats.

To sum up, the state offers diverse habitats from lush green and hilly terrain, to coastal plains and rolling river valleys, criss-crossed by rivers that include the Brahmani, the Mahanadi and the Bansadhara.

*Mahanadi*

## Why are the arts and crafts of Odisha special?

**D**ue to the reigns of many different rulers, the culture, arts and crafts of Odisha underwent many changes, from time to time. Yet, the artistic skill of the Oriya artists remains unparalleled. From traditional times, Odisha has been considered a state blessed with talent for arts. Right from palm leaves writing, to applique work, the craftsmen of Odisha have perfected it all. Several art forms that have died out over time in many parts of the country are still practiced in parts of Odisha.

The craftsmen create breath taking works in silver filigree, wood craft, applique work, brass, and bell metal work. They also excel in horn work, papier mache creations, terracotta figures, and tie and dye textiles. In fact, ever since the Mauryans set textile workshops here, Odisha has been an important hub for the craft of weaving. There are now numerous weaving communities, which have more than 3 lakh weavers. When it comes to music and dance, Odissi music is charming, colourful, and multi-splendoured. In addition to the world renowned Odissi and Chhau dance forms, Odisha boasts of a number of folk dances too.

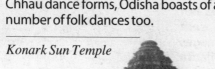

*Konark Sun Temple*

**Konark Dance Festival**
The Konark Sun Temple in Odisha was built in the 13th century. It was conceived as a gigantic solar chariot with twelve pairs of exquisitely-ornamented wheels dragged by seven rearing horses. The exquisite 'natamandir' or the 'dancing hall' of this shrine is an architectural wonder. The Konark Dance Festival is held in December every year, against the beautiful backdrop of this temple.
A host of celebrated classical dancers from all over the country perform in the open-air auditorium. The festival provides a platform for both the performing artistes and the dance connoisseurs to appreciate the essence of various classical dance forms of the country.

# Punjab

Capital : **Chandigarh**
Districts : **22**
Principal Language : **Punjabi**
State Bird : **Eastern Goshawk**
State Animal : **Blackbuck**

*Golden Temple-
Amritsar*

**Golden Temple**

The holiest shrine of the Sikhs is the Golden Temple at Amritsar. The location of the Golden Temple was originally a small lake in a deep forest. It has long been recognized as a place of spiritual significance. It is said that Buddha spent some time there, and later, the first Sikh Guru meditated at the lake. The architecture of the Golden temple represents a unique harmony between Muslim and Hindu styles.

## Why has Punjab seen many divisions in its history?

Punjab, 'the land of five rivers', was one of the centres of the prehistoric Indus valley Civilization. After 1500 BC, it was the site of the earliest Aryan settlements. In the past, Punjab was occupied by Alexander the Great, and then by the Mauryan Empire. Muslims occupied West Punjab by the 8th century, and ushered in Islam. Not until the late 12th century, did they conquer East Punjab, which even

*Punjabi University*

afterward, remained predominantly Hindu. In the late 18th century, the Sikhs rose to dominance. They came into conflict with the British during the early 19th century. In 1849, the British annexed most of the Punjab, and made it a province, though some of the princely states were retained.

With the creation of Pakistan in 1947, Punjab was partitioned according to the prevalence of Muslim and the Hindu populations. The western portion became part of Pakistan. The eastern part stayed with India. The Indian Punjab was divided into three different states on a linguistic basis on November 1st 1966 . The Hindi speaking areas formed the new state of Haryana, while the Northern most districts were transferred to Himachal Pradesh. The remaining regions form present day Punjab.

## What are Punjab's geographical features?

Punjab is bounded on the west by Pakistan, on the north by Jammu and Kashmir, on the northeast by Himachal Pradesh, and on the south by Haryana and Rajasthan. Due to the presence of a large number of rivers, most of the land of Punjab is fertile plain.

However, the south-east region is semi-arid, and Punjab's arid southern border edges the Thar Desert. A belt of swelling hills extends along the northeast at the foot of the Himalayas, and the Shivalik Range rises sharply in the north of the state. Searing summers, torrential monsoons, and cool winters are the climatic conditions of this land.

*Moti Bagh Palace, Patiala*

*National institute of Pharmaceutical Education and Research*

### Why is Punjab known as The 'land of five rivers?'

**T**he name 'Punjab' means 'land of five rivers,' and is derived from the Persian words 'panj,' meaning five, and 'aab,' meaning water. The five rivers of Punjab are the Beas, Chenab, Jhelum, Ravi, and Sutlej. These rivers begin as various small lakes in Himalayas. The Beas merges into the Sutlej at Harike near Ferozepur in Punjab just before crossing the border into west Punjab or Pakistan, where it eventually merges into the river Indus.

The land between the Beas and the Sutlej is called the Doaba. Many important cities are located here. The region between the Beas and Chenab is the heart of Punjab, and is called Majha. The area beyond the Chenab River and around the River Jhelum is Pothohar. Rachna Doab is the name given to the land between the Ravi and Chenab rivers, while east of the river Beas is the area known as Malwa. This region gets its name from a clan called Molois or Malawis that once ruled this area.

States of India

### Bhakra Dam

**T**he Bhakra Dam is India's biggest hydro electric project. It is located near the border of Punjab with Himachal Pradesh. The dam has been constructed across the perennial river Sutlej, which flows down the Shivalik ranges that surrounds the region, and is an engineering marvel. It is one of the highest gravity dams in the world, and it has created a huge reservoir known as the Gobind Sagar reservoir. This dam is virtually the central nervous system of northern India, as it supplies electricity to the entire region.

● *Ninu Dixit*

# Rajasthan

Capital : **Jaipur**
Districts : **33**
Principal Languages : **Hindi, Rajasthani**
State Bird : **Great Indian Bustard**
State Animal : **Chinkara**
State Flower : **Rohida**

## Why is Rajasthan called by this name?

The ancient history of Rajasthan dates back to 1200 AD, when it was a part of different dynasties including the glorious Mauryan Empire. It wasn't until the mid-sixth century that the brave Rajputs, warriors par excellence, came to dominate the region.

Rajasthan was divided into kingdoms, and the valiant Rajputs kept themselves busy with skirmishes amongst the neighbouring kingdoms, or else they faced the Turks, the mighty Sultans of Delhi 's last Sultanate, and later, the Great Mughals. It was around this time that Rajasthan came to be called as Rajputana. Rana Uday Singh, his son Rana Pratap, Bhappa Rawal, Rana Kumbha, and Prithviraj Chauhan were

*Mehrangarh Fort*

some of the most famous Rajput warriors of this time.

Later, most of the regions came under Mughal rule, followed by the Marathas. However, between 1817 and 1818, almost all the princely states in the region entered into alliances with the British. On November 1st 1956, the state of present day Rajasthan came into existence.

*Jaipur*

CURIOUS FACT

**Folk Instruments**

Rajasthan has a great tradition of folk music, and their instruments can be divided into percussion instruments, wind instruments, and string instruments. The dhol, dholak, and nagara are popular percussion instruments, while the common wind instruments are the shehnai and flute, the poongi, the algoza, and the satara. String instruments include a kind of sarangi, while the thali, which is a metal platter, is another popular folk instrument.

*Hawa Mahal Palace*

### Why is the geography of Rajasthan considered unique?

Rajasthan is located in northwest India. It borders Punjab in the north, Haryana and Uttar Pradesh in the northeast, Madhya Pradesh in the east, and Gujarat in the south. Huge areas of the state of Rajasthan consist of the biggest Indian desert-

the Thar Desert. The arid Thar also boasts of Mount Abu, famous for its flora and fauna. While the Aravali Hills provide the much-needed relief to this arid land, the wide spread sand dunes of the desert and arid region make it one of the toughest terrains in the world.

The oldest chain of fold mountains- the Aravalli Range splits the state into two geographical zones- the desert on one side, and the forest belt on the other. The rocky range of Amber, hilly range of Mewar, the river basin of Bharatpur and fertile Aravalli range all combine to make the geography of Rajasthan truly unique.

*Hills around Jaipur*

**Why do we say that industries have played a vital role in Rajasthan's growth?**

Deposits of zinc, copper and other minerals have helped the growth of industry in Rajasthan. The Khetri Copper Complex is the biggest copper plant in India. Mining is a very important industry, and there are about 42 major, and 28 minor mines that provide employment to around 2 million people. Some agricultural products also help industrial growth.

In general, industry in Rajasthan is made up of heavy, medium, and small scale industries, as well as cottage industries and the service industry. The heavy industries include the production of ball bearings and cement, as well as the National Thermal Power Plant in Kota. Small scale industries include ceramics, textiles, block printing, woollen and carpet industry, marble and granite, gems and jewellery. In short, though agriculture is the main occupation of the people, the industrial sector is also very important, as it accounts for about 32.5 per cent of the total share of the state's economy.

I deposited here..
10 Kg copper!

78

# Sikkim

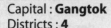

Capital : **Gangtok**
Districts : **4**
Principal Languages : **Lepcha, Bhutia, Limbu, Nepali**
State Bird : **Blood Pheasant**
State Animal : **Red Panda**
State Flower : **Noble Orchid**

*Statue of Guru Rinpoche*

*Rumtek Monastery in Sikkim*

## Why is Sikkim's history different from that of other states?

**S**ikkim was inhabited in pre-historic times by three tribes. They were absorbed by a people known as the Lepcha, who entered Sikkim sometime later. The credit for organizing them into some sort of a society goes to a person called Turve Pa no. Buddhism, the major religion in the state, arrived from Tibet in the 13th century. It took its distinctive Sikkimese form four centuries later, when three Tibetan monks went to Gangtok looking for a certain person whom they

*Kanchenjunga*

## Kanchenjunga

Kanchenjunga in the eastern Himalayas, is situated on the border between Sikkim and eastern Nepal. It is the third highest mountain in the world, and soars to a height of 8586 metres. Its name is derived from four words of Tibetan origin, that can be translated into the Sikkim language as 'five treasuries of the great snow'.

crowned as the first Chogyal or 'Righteous King' of Denzong in 1642. Being the secular and religious head, he was soon recognized by Tibet, and brought sweeping reforms.

After India's independence, Sikkim became a protectorate of India. The role of India became increasingly crucial, with the Chinese military build-up along the northern borders that culminated in an actual invasion early in the 1960's. The king, Palden Thondup Namgyal then gave in to the demands of his people, and Sikkim became the 22nd state of India in 1975.

## What are the main features of Sikkim's geography?

The state of Sikkim has boundaries with Tibet, Nepal, Bhutan, and West Bengal. It is a land of rich and varied scenic beauty, magnificent mountains, eternal snows, dark forests, green fertile valleys, raging torrents and calm, placid lakes. Two principal mountain ranges in Sikkim are the Singilela and Chola. Between these ranges are the main rivers, the Rangit and the Teesta, that are fed by the monsoon rains as well as by melting glaciers.

What a wonderful land this is!

# Tamil Nadu

Capital : **Chennai**
Districts : **32**
Principal Language : **Tamil**
State Bird : **Emerald Dove**
State Animal : **Nilgiri Tahr**
State Flower : **Glory lily**

No Madras patanam, only Madras Presidency.

**Why do we say that the history of Tamil Nadu goes back to ancient times?**

**B**y 300 BC, Tamil Nadu was ruled by three major dynasties-the Cholas, the Pandyas, and the Cheras. This was the classical period of Tamil literature– the Sangam Age – that continued until around AD 300.

The Pallava dynasty rose to power in the 7th and 8th centuries. In the 13th century, with threats of Muslim invasions from the north, the southern Hindu dynasties came together to form the empire of Vijayanagar, which covered all of South India. However, by the 17th century, the Vijayanagar Empire broke up. In 1640, the British negotiated the use of Madraspatnam -now known as Chennai- as a trading post. After independence, the Madras Presidency was disbanded, and Tamil Nadu was established as an autonomous state in 1956.

*Fort St. George*

## Mahabalipuram

**Mahabalipuram is a harbour town founded in the 7th century by the Pallavas in the Kancheepuram district. The harbour of Mahabalipuram traded with the distant kingdoms of South-East Asia. It is famous today for its rock sculptures and temples, which were constructed between 630 and 728 and is a world heritage site.**

## Why is Tamil Nadu called an agricultural state?

Tamil Nadu was historically known for its agriculture from ancient times. In modern times, it has all along been one of the states with a creditable performance in agricultural production. One reason for this is that, the farmers are relatively more responsive, and receptive to changing technologies and market forces. Seventy percent

## Which are the main festivals of Tamil Nadu?

Tamil Nadu celebrates both regional, and religious festivals. Most of the festivals are agrarian in nature, while others have mythological significance. Pongal, a harvest festival, is the most important of all festivals. The Pongal Festival is celebrated for four consecutive days in January. People offer prayers in honour of the Sun God, Air, Water, and Earth. They pray for a good crop and prosperity, and cook a meal called 'Pongal', made of rice, milk and jaggery. The Natyanjali Dance festival is dedicated to Lord Shiva in the form of Nataraja, 'the cosmic dancer'. The festival falls in the month

Happy Pongal!

*Bharat Natyam*

**Tell Me Why**

of the people in Tamil Nadu are engaged in agriculture. Both food crops and cash crops are grown in the state. The major food crops are rice, jowar, ragi, bajra, maize and pulses. The cash crops grown include cotton, sugar cane, coconut, tea and coffee. Other horticultural products like bananas and mangoes are also cultivated. The Department of Agriculture has taken up the challenge to achieve a higher growth rate in agriculture by implementing several development schemes.

of February in the temple city of Chidambaram. The Karthigai Deepam festival is the festival of lights.

The Jallikatu Bull festival is celebrated on the 4th day of Pongal, in Tiruchirapalli. Navarathiri and Deepavali are celebrated with great enthusiasm and zeal. The Chithirai festival is held in the famous Madurai Temples. There is also a famous Music and Dance festival held in Chennai in December.

*Meenakshi Temple*

States of India

*Silk Saree Weaving at Kancheepuram*

### Silk City

**Kancheepuram is located on the Palar River in Tamil Nadu. It is also called the 'city of a thousand temples'. Kancheepuram is famous for its silks too. The silk weavers of Kancheepuram settled here more than 400 years ago, and silk weaving continues to be the main occupation of the people living here. In fact, the silks of Kancheevaram are reputed to be the country's finest.**

# Tripura

Capital : **Agarthala**
Districts : **4**
Principal Languages : **Bengali, Kokborok**
State Animal : **Phayre's Langur**
State Bird : **Green Imperial Pigeon**
State Flower : **Nageshwar**

**Orange Festival**
**T**he Jmpui Hills are the highest hill range of Tripura, and oranges are grown in plenty here. Every year, the unique Orange and Tourism Festival that is held in November, celebrates the bounty of Mother Nature.
● *Hari Rathod*

## What are the physical features of Tripura?

**T**ripura is one of the seven states in the north eastern part of India. It has Bangladesh as its border on its north, west and south. Assam and Mizoram border the eastern part of the state. Tripura is a land of high hills, that are interspersed with river valleys. In the north, it has four valleys, that have been separated by hills with heights of about 1,000 metres. In the south, there is open forestland covering a large area. A wide variety of plant

*Landscape- Tripura*

## Tripura and Tagore

The Nobel laureate Rabindranath Tagore had close relationship with successive Tripura kings. When Tagore was in his 20s, Maharaja Birchandra Manikya Bahadur, a painter, photographer and composer, identified him as a genius. Tagore visited Tripura seven times, and was close to four successive kings.

● *Sneha Rao*

*Ujjayanta Palace, Tripura*

and orchid species are found in the forests of Tripura. Sal is an important product of the forests here. The state is watered by several rivers and their

> I am reading the history of Tripura

tributaries. The Khowati, the Manu, the Haorah, the Muhuri and the Gomati are some important rivers of Tripura. The Gomati is the largest river in the state.

States of India

## How was Tripura formed?

The history of Tripura goes back to ancient times, and it is even mentioned in the epic Mahabharata. The earliest trace of the history of Tripura can be found in the Ashokan pillar inscriptions. Tripura was ruled by the Manikya dynasty from the 14th century. This dynasty had an Indo-Mongolian origin, and ruled Tripura for around 3000 years. With the coming of the colonial era, the Britishers extended their control over Tripura, but granted some independence to the Manikya kings. After the independence of India, Tripura merged with the Indian Union. It became a union territory of the country from November 1st, 1956. On January 21st, 1972, Tripura became an independent state of the Indian Union.

85

## Why are the folk dances of Tripura so interesting?

Tripura has over 19 different tribal communities, as well as Bengali and Manipuri communities. Each community has its own dance forms, which are famous throughout the country.

The Garia dance is performed after sowing seeds in the month of April. It is a time when Tripuris offer prayers to the deity 'Garia' for a bumper harvest. Once the Garia festival ends, the Tripuris and 'Dhukuk'. The Hai Hak dance is performed at the end of the harvesting season by the Halam community of Tripura. The people sing and dance the Wagala Dance after a good harvest. Womenfolk dance, and the theme is 'rehearsal for war'. The Hozagiri dance is a dance in which balancing plays a key role, and it is very different from other tribal dances.

*Tripura- A Landscape*

start waiting for the monsoon. During this period, numerous colourful insects called 'lebang' swarm the hill slopes in search of seeds. These insects are welcomed by Tripuris with the Lebang Boomani Dance.

The people of the Chakma community perform the Bizy dance to welcome the New Year. The dance is accompanied by the sound of flutes known as 'Khenggarang'

Tripura has contributed a lot to Indian culture in terms of folk music. Different types of musical instruments such as the kham, made of wood and animal skin, the sumai which is a flute made of bamboo, sarinda, chongpreng, dangdu and cymbals are used. The state is also well known for its cane and bamboo handicrafts.

86

# Uttarakhand

Capital : **Dehradun**
Districts : **13**
Principal Languages : **Hindi, Garhwali, Kumaoni**
State Bird : **Himalayan Monal**
State Animal : **Himalayan Musk deer**
State Flower : **Brahma Kamal**

## Why is the history of Uttarakhand linked to that of Garhwal and Kumaon?

**T**he history of Uttarakhand is actually the history of two regions, Garhwal and Kumaon. Garhwal was once a part of the Mauryan Empire. In the 15th century, King Ajai Pal merged the 52 principalities of the Garhwal region to form a new kingdom. Garhwal remained a consolidated kingdom for about 300 years. The early medieval history of Kumaon started with the Katyuri dynasty that ruled from 7th to the 11th century. In 1791, the Gurkhas took control of Kumaon, and in 1803, Garhwal also fell to the Gurkhas.

In the 19th century, the British annexed the Gurkha Empire, and along with it, the area that now forms Uttarakhand. Uttarakhand was a part of Uttar Pradesh, and on 9th November 2000, it became the 27th state of Indian union.

CURIOUS FACT

### Valley of Flowers
The Valley of Flowers is a National Park located in the Chamoli district of Uttarakhand. Spread over an area of 87.5 sq kms, the Valley of Flowers offers the visitor the memorable sight of over 500 species of wild flowers blooming in all their glory. This unusual valley is flanked in either side by lofty peaks that remain snow-capped round the year. From November to May, the valley remains under thick layers of snow.

*Bhagirathi River at Gangotri*

### What are the geographical features of Uttarakhand?

The state of Uttarakhand is surrounded by Himachal Pradesh in the north-west, and Uttar Pradesh in the south. It shares its international borders with Nepal and China. The northern part of the state of Uttarakhand is shrouded by Himalayan ranges and glaciers, whereas the lower parts of the state are thickly forested.

*Mindrolling Monastery*

Situated at the height of 7,816 m above sea level, Nanda Devi in the district of Chamoli is the highest point in the state. Two of India's biggest rivers, the Ganga and the Yamuna originate in the glaciers of Uttarakhand. The geography of Uttarakhand is such that it is usually divided into two parts, the western half known as Garhwal, and the eastern region as Kumaon. Did you know that the word Uttarakhand is the Sanskrit term for 'north country'?

That is North Khand.. and this is South Khand.

Tell Me Why

## Nanda Devi National Park

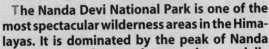

The Nanda Devi National Park is one of the most spectacular wilderness areas in the Himalayas. It is dominated by the peak of Nanda Devi. It is the habitat of several endangered mammals, especially the snow leopard, Himalayan musk deer, and the bharal. The park encompasses the Nanda Devi sanctuary, a glacial basin surrounded by a ring of peaks. The spectacular views, sylvan environment, and richness of the biosphere make it quite different from other parks. The park has been declared a world heritage site by UNESCO.

### Why do tourists flock to Uttarakhand?

Uttarakhand is often called the 'abode of the gods' and it is a popular tourist destination. It is the holiest of all Hindu pilgrimage centres as the land is home to four great religious sites - Gangotri, Yamunotri, Badrinath, and Kedarnath. This apart, Uttarakhand boasts of pristine natural beauty, stately mountains, awe inspiring glaciers and gurgling hill brooks, rare wild life, and opportunities galore for adventure sports.

Nainital, located in the Kumaon foothills, is one of India's most picturesque hill stations surrounded by mountains on three sides. Mussoorie is located in the Garhwal hills. Dehradun is widely known as an important base for trekking and adventure activities. Gangotri is a must for every visitor, as it is located at the source of the holy river Ganges. Uttarakhand also has several glaciers and wildlife sanctuaries which are very famous, like the Jim Corbett National Park, Rajaji National Park, Maktoli Glacier, Nanda Devi Group of Glaciers, and Pindari Glacier.

*Nainital Lake*

# Uttar Pradesh

Capital : **Lucknow**
Districts : **74**
Principal Languages : **Hindi, Urdu**
State Bird : **Sarus Crane**
State Animal : **Swamp Deer**
State Flower : **Palash**

## Why are agriculture and industry important to the economy of Uttar Pradesh?

**U**ttar Pradesh has the second largest economy in India. Agriculture and industry are where the real assets of the state lie. The fertile soil of the state, increased use of fertilizers, better irrigation facilities, and usage of different varieties of high yielding seeds make it one of the major producers of food grains. The major agricultural cultivations are wheat, rice, pulses, oil seeds, sugarcane, and fruits like mangoes and apples.

The major industries are based on minerals, cement manufactur-

*Second Yamuna Bridge, Allahabad*

ing, and small scale units. The region has a large reserve of minerals. There are aluminum units in Banda and Sonbhadra area, copper plants in Pithor garh, Almora Chamoli and Tehri Garhwal, coal reserves in the Singrauli, and limestone deposits in Mirzapur area of the state. Small scale industries also play a major role in the economy of the state.

*Varanasi*

Tell Me Why

## Why is the history of Uttar Pradesh very inspiring?

Uttar Pradesh is the land of the epics- the Mahabharatha and Ramayana. The empire of Chandra Gupta Maurya extended nearly over the whole of Uttar Pradesh. During the Gupta period, the culture and architecture of Uttar Pradesh reached its peak. The decline of the Guptas coincided with the rise of the Huns from Central Asia. The 7th century witnessed the taking over of Kannauj by Harshavardhana.

*Allahabad University*

*Kathak*

In 1526, Babur laid the foundation of the Mughal dynasty. The highlight of the Mughal rule came when Emperor Akbar chose the cities of Agra and Fatehpur Sikri as his capital cities. The Mughal reign saw the construction of some of the most magnificent monuments in Uttar Pradesh. With the emergence of the East India Company, the whole region was captured by the British. Modern-day Uttar Pradesh saw the rise of important freedom fighters on the national scenario. Lal Bahadur Shastri, Jawaharlal Nehru, Smt. Indira Gandhi, and Charan Singh are only a few of the important names who played a significant role in India's freedom movement. During the days of the British Empire, the state was named United Provinces in 1935. This was later changed to Uttar Pradesh in 1950, after India became independent.

**Taj Mahal**
The Taj Mahal, one of the most beautiful monuments in the world, is situated at Agra in Uttar Pradesh. It was built by the Emperor Shah Jahan in memory of his beloved wife Mumtaz Mahal. The Taj mahal has been designated as UNESCO World heritage site.

## How would we describe the geography of Uttar Pradesh?

**U**ttar Pradesh is the fourth largest state of India. It is bounded by Nepal, Himachal Pradesh, Haryana, Rajasthan, Madhya Pradesh and Bihar. The Gangetic Plain occupies three quarters of the state. The entire alluvial plain can be divided into three sub-regions- the eastern, central and western tracts. The Gangetic plain is watered by the Jamuna, the Ganga, and its major tributaries. The Vindhya Hills and plateau in the southern part consists of hard rock strata, with a varied landscape of hills, plains, valleys and plateau. Uttar Pradesh can lay claim to be the oldest seat of India's culture and civilization. The findings of the archaeological exca-

All these books are about Uttar Pradesh..

vations from various places of the state link Uttar Pradesh to the early Stone Age and Harappan era.

The classical dance Kathak, folk arts like Braj Raslila, Ramlila and Charkula are very famous art forms of Uttar Pradesh.

*Fathehpur Sikri*

# West Bengal (Paschim Banga)

Capital : **Kolkata**
Districts : **19**
Principal Language : **Bengali**
State Bird : **White-Throated Kingfisher**
State Animal : **Royal Bengal Tiger**
State Flower : **Night-flowering Jasmine**

*Kolkata High Court*

## What do we know about the history of West Bengal?

In the Vedic Age, Bengal was called 'Vanga'. During the Mahabharatha period, this area was divided into small kingdoms and principalities ruled by chieftains. Around the 3rd century, the Mauryan and the Guptas established their rule. The Palas established their strong rule from about 800 AD till the 11th century, after which the Senas ruled. In the beginning of the 13th century, Bengal became a part of the Delhi Sultanate and later the Mughal Empire.

The nearness to the sea also saw many foreigners reaching these shores- the Portuguese, the Dutch, the French, the Danish, and the British. The British ultimately captured power in Bengal. In 1905, they partitioned Bengal on the basis of religion. Kolkata remained the capital till 1911. In 1947 when India became independent, Bengal was partitioned between India and Pakistan. India's share came to be known as West Bengal, and Pakistan's share was called East Pakistan.

The Bay of Bengal is the way to Bengal.

## Why is Bengal proud of its rich cultural heritage?

*Eden Gardens Stadium*

West Bengal's culture is distinguished by its festivals, music, cinema, drama and literature. Being the land of Bankim Chandra, Rabindranath and Aurobindo, West Bengal is said to be the birth place of modern Indian literature.

The theatre in Bengal dates back to 18th century. Theatre gained prominence during the freedom struggle of India, when it was used as a tool of expression. Girishchandra Ghosh, Rabi Roy, Sisir Bhaduri, Badal Sircar, Shobha Sen and Soumitra Chatterjee are some of the prominent names in Bengali theatre. When it comes to contemporary cinema, the immense contribution of the great Bengali director Satyajit Ray cannot be ignored. Music and dances are also integral parts of the Bengali culture. The people of Bengal are closely associated with Rabindra Sangeet, Rabindra Nritya Natya, which consists of songs and song-dance sequences composed by Tagore, and Nazrul Geeti, or songs by Kazi Nazrul Islam. Folk dances and songs are also popular. Bankura's famed handmade pottery, especially the decorated horse, is a traditional craft. The biggest festival in the state is Durga Puja.

*All India Radio, Kolkata*

Tell Me Why

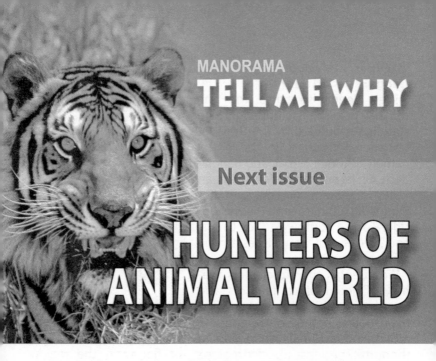

96

## Why is the geography of West Bengal a varied one?

West Bengal stretches from the Himalayas to the Bay of Bengal. The state is surrounded by the three international frontiers in the north, namely, Bhutan, Nepal, and Bangladesh. On its northeast, lies the green valley of Assam. On the east lies Bangladesh. Bihar lies on the western side. To the southwest, lies Orissa, and the Bay of Bengal lies to the south of West Bengal.

West Bengal, therefore, offers a variety of geographical features. The State has the alluvial plains known as the Dooars in the south, and the mountainous Himalayan region in the north. The dense wooded regions in the Dooars have rich and varied flora and fauna. The Malda region, irrigated by the river Mahananda constitutes the fertile mid section.

The alluvial plains in the south are the basin of the River Damodar, also known as the 'river of Bengal's sorrow'. The name was coined after a number of floods in the region were attributed to the river. The other main rivers are the Ganga and Hoogly. The district of 24 Parganas has pristine forests known as the Sundarbans.

No more 'Pondi'. Only Puducherry!

FROM FRANCE

*Howrah Bridge*

Next issue

# HUNTERS OF ANIMAL WORLD

### Movements For New States

**T**he main movements today for separate statehood are the Telangana movement, and the movement for the separate state of Gorkhaland. The Telangana Movement refers to a movement to support the creation of a new state of Telangana from the existing state of Andhra Pradesh. For more than 400 years, Telangana was part of Hyderabad state. Telangana became a part of Andhra Pradesh in 1956.

Gorkhaland is the name given to the area around Darjeeling and the Dooars in north West Bengal. During the 1980s, Subash Ghisingh raised the demand for the creation of the country called Gorkha. In 2008, a new party called Gorkha Janmukti Morcha has raised the demand for Gorkhaland once again.

Lakshadweep doesn't have a lakh of Islands.

## Chandigarh

The Union Territory of Chandigarh is the 1$^{st}$ planned modern city of India.

Chandigarh serves as the joint capital of both Punjab and Haryana.

## Delhi

Delhi is different from other union territories, that it was created by the National Capital Territory Act of 1991, which makes it a National Capital territory or NCT. Delhi has always been a historic city, in ancient, medieval and modern times.

## Union Territories

1. Andaman and Nicobar Islands
2. Chandigarh
3. Dadra and Nagar Haveli
4. Daman and Diu
5. Lakshadweep
6. Puducherry
7. Delhi (National Capital Territory)

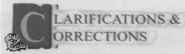

# CLARIFICATIONS & CORRECTIONS

*It is our policy to correct errors, and present differing views and clarifications about the contents in previous issues. Please send in your feedback, mentioning the title and page number.*

Anjana Trivedi, a teacher from Mumbai, has pointed out an error in our February issue, 'Evolution'.

She writes that on Page 26, it is given that, 'the duck billed platypus is a strange looking bird' which is not correct. The duck billed platypus is considered as a mammal that lays eggs.

She also provides an add-on information- an international consortium of scientists, has decoded the genome of the duck billed platypus. This gene map proves that platypus is part bird, mammal and reptile.

An analysis of the genome, published in the journal 'Nature', can help scientists piece together a more complete picture of the evolution of all mammals, including humans.

*Thank you Anjana, for your valuable feedback.*

*- Editor*

# I Wonder Why?
### The question of the month

Aren't there many little things you have wondered about, but didn't know whom to ask? Send us your questions, and we will give you the fascinating reasons behind the incredible mysteries of life.

### Why does boiling milk overflow, but boiling water does not?

**P**robably due to the fat molecules in milk. The fat separates from the thinner, watery liquid and as the water in the milk boils, the steam rises, and this milk fat layer moves up. You can prevent the boiling over problem by lowering the heat. When milk is boiled, a membrane-like film containing cream and casein is formed. When milk begins to boil, the heat energy is used for the conversion of water into steam. As a result, the pressure below the film increases suddenly and the rising bubbles of steam makes the milk overflow.

The major component of milk is water (83%). Its other constituents are protein (5%), sugar (5%), and fat (7%). When heated, fat being lighter than water, floats as a creamy layer on the top, and water vapour, in the form of steam bubbles, is trapped under it. Further heating results in the formation of more number of bubbles. These bubbles expand, and lift the creamy layer, causing it to overflow. In the case of water, the steam bubbles break as they reach the surface. So boiling water does not overflow.

● *K.P. Sukumar*

It's our luck, milk is overflowing!

| MANORAMA TELL ME WHY - STATES OF INDIA | |
|---|---|
| Editor: Ammu Mathew | Editor-in-Charge: N.M. Mohanan* |
| Printed and Published by V. Sajeev George, on behalf of M.M. Publications Ltd, P.B. No. 226, Kottayam - 686 001 at M.M. Publications Ltd, P.B. No. 226, Kottayam - 686 001 and Malayala Manorama Press, Kottayam - 686 039 and published from M.M. Publications Ltd, P.B. No. 226, Kottayam - 686 001. | |
| * Responsible for selection of news under the PRB Act | |

April 2012 ₹ 20   MANORAMA TELL ME WHY   ISSN 0975 - 0436
KERENG/2006/18236 Registered Reg. No. KL/KTM/656/2010-12  KL/CR/KTM/WPP -1/ 2010-12
Licensed to post without prepayment

# Your child is growing up in the mouse age.

**A**n age in which even play is a deliberate act of growing up. An age in which the mouse plays supreme. Yet, there are things which the electronic mouse is not capable of.

It cannot enjoy a story read aloud for the nth time;
- run about, with a just-learnt rhyme on the lips;
- get excited over a puzzle solved;
- splash colours and yell with joy.

Bring your child to the wonder world of MAGIC POT

Where fantasy merges with real-time enjoyment & learning.
And growing up becomes a funtime activity.

HIDE 'N' SEEK

Somebody is hiding on top of the house. olour the dotted ts of the picture nd see who it is.

FOR NURSURY / PRIMARY SCHOOL CHILDREN

**MagicPot**

M. M. Publications Ltd., P.B. No. 226,
Kottayam - 686 001, Kerala, India.
Ph: 0481-2563721-22-23, Fax: ++91-481-2564393.
E-Mail : Editorial Division: childrensdivision@mmp.in
Subscription Division: subscription@mmp.in

# TELL ME WHY

₹ 20

# STATES OF INDIA

9 770975 043005

## 100 + FACTS ABOUT OUR STATES